NATURE, GRACE, AND RELIGIOUS DEVELOPMENT

NATURE, GRACE AND RELIGIOUS DEVELOPMENT

by Barry McLaughlin, S.J.

The Newman Press • *Westminster, Maryland*
1964

to Thomas P. Gavigan, S.J.

Second Printing, September, 1964

Imprimi potest: JOHN M. DALEY, S.J.
     Provincial of the Maryland Province

Nihil obstat: JOHN F. DEDE, S.S.
    Censor Deputatus

Imprimatur: LAWRENCE J. SHEHAN
    Archbishop of Baltimore
    May 15, 1963

Introduction

The most serious weakness of the human mind is its inability to sustain awareness of the greatest of realities. Man fidgets before the obvious. Truth bores him. Yet God's grace and His love, His justice, and His mercy are true. They constitute the nucleus of truth, the most basic of realities. Man's wisdom consists in his ability to perceive life against the background of these supernatural realities which, even more than natural realities, even more than suffering and joy and death, are at the heart of his destiny.

The dimensions of religious experience—the religious man's encounter with God, with men, with the things of creation—these express most fully the reality of life. Merely to regard this reality psychologically, to submit it to empirical investigation, renders it unreal. For the methodology of science brackets God and consequently confuses the real and the illusory, the saint and the psychotic.

Yet science sharpens man's vision of reality. The contemporary interest in the social sciences—particularly in psychology—has prompted general agreement in theological writing that faith in supernatural reality is strongest and most personally meaningful when it functions in a mature, well-balanced, emotionally healthy personality. Often on a practical level it has been found necessary to reconstruct the natural, psychological facets of personality before the foundations can be laid for a fully mature supernatural life. There have been neurotic and semi-neurotic saints (just as there are emotionally mature individuals who are spiritual neurotics). But these are the exceptions.

This interest in the psychological aspects of religious life has produced the literature of ascetical psychology. Writers in this area have attempted to achieve a systematic integration, theoretically and practically, of ascetical and psychological considerations, emphasizing especially psychological dimensions.

Several themes have recurred with some frequency in this literature.[1] First, there is an increasing recognition that capacity for spiritual development is to a great extent conditioned by natural intellectual endowments. Generally speaking, the individual of superior intelligence is also capable of greater sensitivity, greater self-knowledge, and consequently greater perfection than his less intelligent counterpart. Though this need not be necessarily true, God generally uses His instruments according to their natural abilities.

In addition, there is widespread agreement that a lack of understanding of the nature of volitional activity and of the proper methods of training the will have hindered the spiritual development of many religious. Authors in contemporary ascetical psychology consequently stress the psychology of will in their writings. In particular, they insist that the will is not a muscle, that motives are not developed merely by the repetition of external actions, but rather through the deliberate cultivation of intellectual values.

Another well-established principle of ascetical psychology states that the spiritual life is closely related to the condition of a person's health. Weariness, headaches, nervous tension can be of profit for spiritual growth, but can also

[1] Joseph P. Fisher, S.J., "Nature and Grace," *Review for Religious*, 13 (1954), 146–147.

block progress and interfere with the individual's apostolic work.

Writers have also pointed out that, in general, the possession of natural virtues greatly facilitates the exercise of supernatural virtues and gives them solidity. The individual who is by nature or training thoughtful of others will benefit from this natural endowment in his effort to practice the virtue of supernatural charity. Functionally, all virtues, even supernatural ones, are dependent upon natural virtues.

Unfortunately, few authors have been concerned with problems of the dynamics of personality development. This lacuna is present in the literature of ascetical psychology primarily because until recently little theoretical or empirical concern has been given by psychologists to the processes and stages of growth characteristic of adulthood. Typically, developmental studies cease with adolescence. A great wealth of literature is available on childhood and adolescence, but only within the past few years have analyses appeared which are concerned primarily with the problems of young adulthood and middle age. Consequently, because ascetical psychology is chiefly concerned with these stages of life, little integration of the dynamics of religious life and the developmental aspects of personality theory has been achieved.

The present book is an approach to such an integration. Its inspiration derives from the theoretical formulations recently elaborated by a leading theorist of personality development—Erik H. Erikson. The theory deals specifically with the developmental patterns of adult life and hence provides a basis for treating, psychologically, the dynamic features of religious growth.

The orientation of this book is therefore psychological, rather than theological. An attempt is made to supply a coherent psychological account of the process of spiritual growth and of the crises attending this process. Relatively little attention is given to dogmatic and scriptural theology. For this reason the book should be complemented by a more specifically theological treatment.[2]

Yet it is invalid to sharply dichotomize the reality of religious life into theological and psychological categories. The natural permeates the supernatural and is permeated by it. Grace and nature co-operate in man. This is the central lesson of the Incarnation. God took upon Himself man's human nature and, consequently, that nature has been elevated and made to function as a channel of grace. Nature never initiates the activity of grace, but since God has Himself implanted laws in nature, it is logical to suppose that He will follow the natural patterns operative in the human personality when He works through grace.[3] Since Christ has dignified human nature, the aim of any natural growth process is transformed: "So that we shall reach perfect manhood, that maturity which is proportioned to the complete growth of Christ" (Eph. 4:13).

[2] For example, Joseph de Guibert, S.J., *The Theology of the Spiritual Life* (New York: Sheed and Ward, 1953); or August Brunner, S.J., *A New Creation* (New York: The Philosophical Library, 1956); or René Carpentier, S.J., *Life in the City of God* (New York: Benziger, 1959).

[3] Dominic W. Maruca, S.J., "Nature and Vocations," *The Theologian*, 14 (1958), 89.

Contents

NATURE, GRACE, AND RELIGIOUS DEVELOPMENT

Vocation

1 The conditions of contemporary life anesthetize the religious sensitivity of modern man. This at least is the contention of many religious leaders and cultural critics. They argue that the greatest marvel of the present age, a marvel which far surpasses modern science and its wonders, is that man has learned to maintain, comfortably and amiably, an attitude of blissful resignation—a resignation which Thoreau characterized as quiet desperation. Modern man has learned to live with his despair. But to do this he has had to invent new and flattering masks to conceal his distress—above all, from himself.

These masks have been described in the writings of many Catholic and Protestant theologians. There is, for example, the mask of intellectual superiority which is often worn by atheistic scientists. Denying all spiritual realities, such men answer all questions with a slide rule, measure all values numerically. They have one religion, that of science, and maintain an unquestioning assurance in its dogmas. Whatever cannot be analyzed experimentally and quantitatively does not exist.

Another mask expresses proud defiance. It is worn by hopeless men who suffer the anguish of personal insignificance while masquerading as modified Nietzschean supermen. For such men true dignity consists in the realization that there is nothing beyond the material world. Flung at

1

random upon the earth, man fashions himself, his life, as
best he may. Values are dead, and so is God. However,
there is no Nietzschean optimism in the unlimited possi-
bilities of the superman. There is merely the effort to be
honest in the face of the meaningless joke which is life.

Another, more common mask of modern man shows an
expression of happy contentment amid material prosperity.
It is the most popular form of concealment in American
culture. Beneath this mask the theologian recognizes the
materialist neurosis—a syndrome of emptiness, boredom,
apathy, despair. The therapy prescribed—actually enforced
—by contemporary American culture is distraction. But
while it is the only thing which consoles him, distraction is
the greatest of man's miseries. Man is fleeing in an effort to
shake off the omnipresent dust of his boredom. He runs to
avoid the terrible vision of his despair. As long as he flees,
he is safe. The dust of his boredom goes unnoticed. The
specter of despair does not haunt him. But as soon as he
stops, the dust is there coating his hands and his feet; and
he stares into eyes which mirror his own bleak despair. For
without God nothing has meaning.

To aid him in his flight from boredom, man has fabri-
cated the world of noise. His greatest fear is the fear of
silence. In the judgment of some philosophers, man's miraculous technology has been exploited chiefly to eliminate
silence. The babel of radio and television saturates the
mind with distractions—news items, bits of irrelevant information, sentimental music or semi-musical noise, trivial
drama that dulls taste.[1] Advertising is seen to be deliberately calculated to artificially intensify materialistic crav-
ings, to deaden spiritual affections, and consequently to set
barriers between the human soul and its divine Origin.

[1] Max Picard, *The Flight from God* (Chicago: Regnery, 1951), p. 1.

Human life, it is said, is becoming depraved, fundamentally corrupt.

Religious writers contend that the root of this corruption grows out of the unreality of modern life. They contend that modern values are posited upon an unnatural principle: the ultimate worth of the merely material. Man has become the servant of material things, of the gods of the plastic age. He has been made to serve mammon. The end of productivity is not man and his elevation, but merely affluence. There are no ultimates, except this one supreme value of material abundance. The modern world is shaping man in a fundamentally inhuman way, and the frenzy it imposes upon him has but one effect—man is prevented from remembering God. Modern man has forgotten that he flees from God.

In this flight man is said to be alienated from himself, from his fellow men, and from nature. He is being transformed into an automaton, blindly seeking to find security in the herd where individual thought, feeling, and action are submerged. Yet while he strives to lose himself in the mob, to cling as closely as possible to other members of the herd, man remains essentially alone, pervaded by a deep sense of insecurity, anxiety, and guilt. The palliatives which society offers to alleviate this sense of isolation—the strict routine of bureaucratized, mechanical work, the deadening routine of forced amusement—these rob man of the most fundamental of human desires, the human longing for transcendence, and leave him dejected, on the brink of neuroticism. For in his isolation modern man becomes aware that he has lost selfhood, that he is an automaton and, like the neurotic, does not know how to love.[2]

[2] Erich Fromm, *The Art of Loving* (New York: Harper, 1956), pp. 86–87.

Yet, paradoxically, in an age when men are apparently losing their selfhood, when many theologians and religious leaders decry man's dehumanization, an emphasis unique in history is placed on man's individuality, his personal worth. The dignity of the human person, his capacity for self-determination, his fundamental uniqueness—these concepts, always part of the Judeo-Christian tradition, are central in today's secular drama, art, literature, philosophy, and in modern culture generally.

Perhaps the psychologists would view this paradox as a reaction against the depersonalization inherent in modern life. From a cold, meaningless universe, man has turned inside to the self, to the realization that to himself he is the most important person in the world. He may realize dimly that it would not make the slightest difference to the universe if he had never existed, yet he represses this intuition and clings to its counterpart—to the intuition that he is at the center of a unique, living network of relationships, experiences, and influences.

Existentialist literature especially has emphasized this side of the paradox of modern life. In all of its forms contemporary existentialism stresses the ultimate value of the person, his selfhood, and above all his liberty to decide what he is to be, his self-determination. Man is more than an automaton. He is free to choose for himself, and must choose, in his present context, with full responsibility and with full willingness to take the consequences. The one element that makes man a man is his freedom. It is in his free choices that man can hope to achieve authenticity.

The quest for authenticity characterizes modern art. It is a motif that echoes through modern literature. Yet the critique of the theologian retains its validity. The mass of men lack the perception of the artist. They continue wearily in their flight. They are searching for meaning, for authenticity, but they search as though blind, stumbling from one painful pleasure to another. The more perceptive author or playwright senses and portrays modern man's quest for authenticity—for an authenticity that must be remade moment by moment in the individual's act of decision, in that act of decision which cuts the individual off from the world of flight.

When this incisive action is performed, however, man finds himself alone, confronts himself—and his egoism. He sees that he is unique as a person—that he has undergone unique experiences, that he has suffered and borne his own wounds, that he is the product of a unique pattern of environmental, educational, and social forces, and that these impose upon him certain conventions of behavior. And if he is authentic, such a man sees in the same moment his nothingness. He is locked in himself, unable to move out to others without faith. He is an individual, but a meaningless individual, inconsequential and self-centered—unless there is some value which gives him value, unless there is something, someone beyond himself in whom he can believe. The awareness of individuality carries with it the grotesque vision of egoism and unauthenticity—"and the last state of that man becomes worse than the first" (Matt. 12:45).

For the root of individuality, that which gives man personal significance and genuine worth, is beyond man. An act of faith is required to come to grips with this reality. In this act of faith, belief in oneself is asserted by affirming oneself in God. Belief in God provides the basis for belief in oneself and in other men who possess in God the root and center of their existence. Without such faith there is only egoism—egoism precisely because man recognizes his true value and worth and yet is incapable and unwilling to make the act of faith that allows him to perceive the value of others. Every human being is the independent center of living forces, capable of infinite perfection because he is capable of possessing absolute Truth. In this sense, absolute self-assertion and self-estimation does not imply egoism. It is the refusal to recognize and attribute this same significance to others that is the fundamental characteristic of the egotist. Man escapes egoism only in that act of faith whereby he recognizes that all men are sons of the same Father and consequently brothers.

Affirmation of God and affirmation of fellow man—these provide the only authentic solution to the riddle of modern life. The alternatives—as contemporary religious writers have pointed out—are a meaningless, inhuman automatism, hectic flight, self-centered pride. But affirmation of God and man demands the attitude of faith, and this is not man's natural attitude. Faith is the gift of the Father. Gradually God draws man on. The human spirit, in its most profound and original orientation, is directed, not toward the self, but toward God, toward the "wholly other."

This is why man becomes himself only by existing more intensely, only by basing his life upon values that surpass the narrow limits of his own existence. Self is not effaced before an impersonal ideal. On the contrary, man recognizes the full potentiality of his personality by an adhesion to the Source of all personality.[3] Man establishes himself, realizes his potential, to the extent that he turns himself to God and situates himself before the eyes of God. Participating in the love of God, man is called to attain to the perfection of his personality.

God calls man to love. It is a call to generosity, to a direct love of value in all its plenitude. Some men ignore the call. Other men respond imperfectly. They love with a love that restricts its horizons to the narrow limits of the finite self.

[3] Robert O. Johann, S.J., *The Meaning of Love* (Westminster: Newman, 1955), p. 42.

Their love excludes other selves, and to this extent never
attains plenitude. But there are other men who respond
fully. They have learned that love demands absolute generosity, that charity requires total selflessness. Love embraces all men or it is not love at all. Ideally, such a love
characterizes the man of God.

Religious experience allows of many gradations. For a
great many people religion is primarily a matter of routine
and is expressed in conventions accepted on the authority
of someone else. In childhood the average person in American society assimilates the religious practices of his parents
through a process of conditioning and imitation. Later, especially in adolescence, there may be doubts and difficulties;
but these are rarely faced with prolonged sincerity and are
soon forgotten. Many men never consider seriously the
process by which they have gained their convictions.
Reasoning is often merely a process of finding arguments
for what is already held. In matters of faith this is especially true. The basis of religious faith and the content of
personal belief are, for some, matters of intellectual conviction, of personal meditation and meaningful reflection.
But for many in our society they are matters of emotion, of
blind, unreflective faith.

This at least was the opinion of William James, who was
convinced that while for some few it exists as an acute
fever, religion is for most men a dull habit. The typical
churchgoer has probably never felt the remotest approach
to a religious experience, however thorough his performance of the duties which his church enjoins. This point
may be debated, especially in the Church where grace can
supply for human deficiency. Nevertheless, it is most
likely true that there are many people who are psychologically and spiritually incapable of religious experience—

of an authentic inner experience of God and of His call, of His right to their personal lives.

For those who are capable and who have been touched by grace, religious experience originates in an experience of discovery. It is an experience, essentially, of surprise. There is a moment of inspiration, of intuition. And there is always a subsequent sense of urgency.

In many respects, such an experience resembles the aesthetic experience of the artist. The artist may, for example, be walking in a field, when all at once nature strikes him in a quite new aspect. He finds it extraordinary that things should be as they are. This happened to the painter Monet as a young man.[4] He suddenly saw the fields, not as solid flat objects covered with grass or useful crops and dotted with trees, but as colors in astonishing variety and subtlety of gradation. He was surprised and attracted. It was an exciting and compelling discovery, especially since it was a discovery of something real, something independent of Monet himself. This was half of the pleasure—the pleasure of discovering a truth about the real. And the urgency it conveyed derived from the compelling need to express this truth, to communicate it to others.

The religious intuition carries with it the same sense of surprise and even more urgency. Chesterton describes St. Francis of Assisi emerging from a cave after his conversion and suddenly finding that the world was upside down.[5] The trees of the forest and the towers of the town hung head downward as in a pool. In that instant St. Francis realized perfectly the absolute dependence of all things upon God. He was overwhelmed with a sense of gratitude. God from all eternity held the world. Nothing had been dropped.

[4] Joyce Cary, *Art and Reality* (New York: Harper, 1958), p. 1.
[5] Gilbert K. Chesterton, *St. Francis of Assisi* (New York: Doubleday, 1924), p. 109.

This was the intuition which transformed his life. He would now see the trees of the forest, the town, the birds, all things in a new and divine light, as eternally in danger, in breathtaking dependence upon God.

Another saint, Ignatius of Loyola, speaking in the third person in his autobiography, described an experience typical of the insight of the religious man: "It was his greatest consolation to gaze upon the heavens and the stars, which he often did, and for long stretches at a time, because when doing so he felt within himself a powerful urge to be serving the Lord."[6] Certainly not all men are capable of such insight. Few follow it to its logical conclusion, to the complete and total dedication of their lives to the service of God. For the religious vocation, as an absolute commitment, involves what Kierkegaard termed the movement of the absurd. This movement is not a flight from the world or from the things of the world and the sufferings of men. Rather it is a consecration of the things of the world and the sufferings of men in an attitude of faith.

The development of a religious vocation is proportioned to the individual's faith. As this faith develops and its dimensions are revealed, the necessity for total and unwavering commitment becomes more and more apparent. The quest for authenticity, characteristic of the modern world, is characteristic of the religious man as well. In fact, the desire for authenticity constitutes his fundamental moral orientation. And it is in the life of faith that he realizes best an authentic mode of existence. For him authenticity demands and is faith.

Christian faith is the ability to think the thoughts of Christ. It is marked by mental communion with Christ, by

[6] *St. Ignatius' Own Story*, trans. William J. Young, S.J. (Chicago: Regenery, 1956), pp. 11–12.

participation in divine Truth. In hope the Christian enters
into the purpose of the Father as it is unfolding in his life.
Hope is a confident participation in the divine Will, a
conscious and deliberate trust in the divine plan. Love is a
surrender to the rhythm of God's love. It is a participation
in that Charity in which alone human love finds refuge and
healing. But hope and love are rooted in faith. It is faith
which transforms man's thinking. Faith transforms his intentions so that he becomes capable of hope. It transforms
his love so that he becomes receptive to the redemptive fire
of God's love. And faith, like hope and charity, derives its
meaning from the cross and resurrection of Christ.

The initial insight of faith concerns man's purpose in existing. Man lives to praise God in hope and love, to rever-
ence Him in humility, to serve Him in gratitude. The
ordinary Sunday Christian realizes this. He will admit that,
when one faces essentials, it is God alone that matters. But
he lets it rest at that. There has been no intuition; there
is no sense of urgency. The man of God, prompted by grace,
takes this one comprehensive truth and explores its implications. Somehow this insight carries with it for the religious
man the compelling recognition of the need for sanctity.

The impetus to sanctity originates in the desire for God
and for His pleasure. "Thou hast made us for Thyself, O
Lord, and our hearts are restless till they rest in Thee." If
man did not possess this desire, this yearning for God, then
it would be possible for him to thrive in hell. But, in fact,
He alone is sufficient for man who made him. And all the
things of creation are given man to help him to satisfy this
need for God.

Creatures are placed along man's way so that he, their
fellow creature, can use them and with them find the way
to God. The chief concern of the religious man is not to
find pleasure or success, life or health or money or rest, or

even things like virtue and wisdom. Still less does he seek
to find their opposites—pain, failure, death, or sickness.
But in all that happens he has learned to seek the will of
God. In this alone can man give back God's love and himself with it.

As long as there is the possibility that this surrender of
self is incomplete, as long as there is an attachment to some
one of God's creatures, there is a pull in the wrong direction. The religious man must be capable of complete concentration, of complete attention to God and the will of
God. As long as there is attachment to something outside of
God's will, attention is lost. It may not be a question of sin.
It is simply that the picture of reality is slightly crooked.
And nothing is quite as distracting as a crooked picture.

Yet the attitude of detachment from the things of this
world carries with it an intrinsic risk. Man cannot love well
enough the creatures of God. The love of the children of
light for the creatures of this world should surpass the love
of the children of darkness. The man of God runs a great
risk in not loving things enough. Too little love for God, for
oneself, for other men—these lead to a disordered love of
the pleasures and comforts of creation and the inability to
find revealed in creatures the God who gave them.

The first moment, then, in the progression through faith
to sanctity is the moment of detachment. It is, however, a
detachment which terminates ultimately in far greater love
for God's creatures. The first great directive that the religious man discovers is that man's activity is to be ordered
to the praise and service of God. Man is truly free to choose
or to reject God. The Fall did not simply happen long ago,
but is an existential reality in man's everyday life. Each
man re-enacts the situation of Adam: each man stands
naked to choose or not to choose the will of God.

Refusal is basically pride, and this is the worst sin—the

basis, in fact, of all sin. Pride is the positive assertion of
self over God as the supreme object of one's love and action.
As the worst sin it is also the most ridiculous. To assert himself before God, man must borrow from God the energy to
defy Him. No sin is its own contradiction so patently, and
no sin is therefore so great a break with reality.

Yet all sin is a break with reality—more or less severe.
It is a refusal to return God's love. Man has within himself
the power to avoid conspicuous acts of sin. Mere social
pressure often restrains him. But the evil is only repressed
to emerge in more subtle ways—in spiritual complacency,
vanity, secret pride. The world does not condemn hidden
sins as forcefully as it condemns shameful, external sins.
But Christ forgave public sinners and condemned the
Pharisees because their sins were less compatible with love.

Conversion to God is therefore dependent upon a man's
attitude of detachment and humility. Once these virtues are
present, there can be progress in faith. The attitude of
humility complements the attitude of detachment. A
humble man finds nothing unholy, nothing evil in itself.
Creation cannot be separated from God. The religious man
sees that to save for God what belongs to Him, he must give
to the world what belongs to the world. The service of God
consists in giving one direction to all of one's efforts, in
sanctifying this world and bringing it to God.

In its development the religious vocation has two addi-
tional moments—these concern the call and the response to
the call. The call is personal and an invitation to a personal
relationship. This is the universal law of all religion and of
all heroism generally—that a man who towers over his
generation possesses the capacity to compel other men to
trample on their selfish interests and to devote themselves
completely to his cause. And in an age where heroes are

discredited, Christ still possesses this capacity to arouse the
desire to imitate and follow. For Christ is alive today among
men. Men will either love or hate Him, but few will ignore
Him. Many men of the past have had this capacity to
arouse in their fellows love of an extreme intensity—
Socrates in his disciples, Julius Caesar in his legionaries,
Napoleon in his soldiers. But today these men belong to the
dim past. No one would give his life or his possessions for
them; few men would even be willing to make a slight
sacrifice for their memory or for the principles they ad-
vocated. No one curses Socrates or Caesar or Napoleon, even
though many promote ideals diametrically opposed to
theirs. But with Christ it is different. Christ is still loved
and still cursed. Men still renounce their possessions for His
sake and even surrender their lives for love or hatred of
Him.

Christ was and is a sign of contradiction. His call still
goes out to men. Not all Christians heed the call. Few are
willing to face up to its consequences. Yet apart from
Christ, as Pascal wrote, man knows neither what his life
nor his death is; he does not know what God is or what he
himself is. This is the fundamental premise of Christianity
—that Christ is the final ideal for man on earth. Without
Christ, in the words of Dostoevski, everything in the world
becomes filth and sin.

Man has an intrinsic desire to be at ease. He resists all
that would take him out of his usual element. In a dynamic,
evolving universe, man alone refuses to consent to change.
He fashions a human religion for himself and seeks a
human salvation proportioned to his human standards. The
Gospel's paradoxes are wine too strong for most men. Man
lacks courage and refuses to acknowledge the Christian
revelation that all forms of death are necessary gates to life.
There is an austerity and a heroism demanded by the call

of Christ, and most men lack the appetite for austerity and shrink before heroism. They would rather be left alone.

"Not my will but thine be done" (Luke 22:42). This sentence contains the essence of Christian austerity and heroism. Christ's austerity did not imply a flight from the world, from its riches and pleasures. Nor does it necessarily connote the abnegation of which the mystics spoke. The austerity of Christ and all of His heroism consisted in an inward, reverent, and strong willing of all that His heavenly Father willed. For Christ, the only reality in all existence, in every event, was the Father's will. In all circumstances and under every contingency, He pierced to this ultimate fact—that there was absolutely nothing that was not controlled by the will of God.

This attitude is one of the inward man, one which is perceptible only to the man himself. And it is an act which must be constantly renewed, so often in fact as the imperative or permissive will of God is seen in the happenings of life. In its outward manifestation it is something quite simple, yet it is an act requiring force, a thing which demands courage.[7]

Total and loving dedication to the Father's will—this is the essence of Christ's teaching and the central element in His call. Christ wills that men respond generously and absolutely to this call. Not all men are called to a life formally religious, but all are called to share in Christ's joys and sufferings and thereby to effect the salvation of the world. This is the beginning of all wisdom: "Come to me, all you who labor and are burdened, and I will give you rest. Take my yoke upon you and learn of me, for I am meek and humble of heart; and you will find rest for your souls" (Matt. 11:28–29).

[7] Karl Adam, *The Son of God* (New York: Sheed and Ward, 1934), p. 27.

The moment of response is a moment of surrender, absolute commitment, total dedication. On a very practical level, this means that there is nothing selfish or egotistical left, that personal wishes may be curbed at will, that Christ is all. The life of union with Christ means the perfect loss of self. This, of course, is the highest sanctity and is not achieved easily or all at once. It demands a steady and determined effort to hold Christ in the center of attention—to measure by His standards, to think His thoughts, to value His values.

The greatest obstacle at this point, that which does most to prevent a generous response to the call of Christ and consequent sanctity, is the lack of an interior life. If Christ's standards are to be man's standards, His values man's values, then man must come into prayerful contact with Christ—with the historical Christ that he might learn of Him and assimilate His mentality, with the glorious Christ that he might derive from His merits the graces needed to be faithful to his calling. Contemplation of Christ sanctifies man. For Christ in all of His actions was teaching. The goal of the religious man's interior life must be to establish himself in the presence of Christ. It is not a discursive process, but a process in which the individual forgets himself and allows himself to be caught up in Christ, in His actions, and in His attitudes. It does not terminate in a carefully planned scheme of perfection, but in communion with the Son of God. "For we do not know what we should pray for as we ought, but the Spirit himself pleads for us with unutterable groanings" (Rom. 8:26).

In addition to formal prayer and contemplation, the fullness of interior life demands the continual attitude of recollection. This attitude is an orientation toward the things of the world rather than a turning away from them. True recollection does not consist in banishing all thoughts of everyday matters, but in thinking of them within the context provided by faith. For all things tell of God if man is attentive enough to hear them speak.

The terminal point of the process by which man responds through faith to the divine invitation is attained only at death. For the response to grace is never complete until a man can do no more for God. There are, however, several critical moments in this process of supernatural development: the initial moment of detachment and humility, the moment of the call, and the moment of the response. These have been discussed briefly in the preceding pages. They are by no means to be understood as temporal durations. Perhaps in an individual case, all three moments coalesce. Generally speaking, however, the essence of the personal vocation of the man of God is contained in such a process of supernatural development. The individual normally realizes the full implications of his vocation only after several, perhaps many, years of service in the cause of Christ. A complete and mature response to the call of Christ is generally possible only after the initial flush of generosity has passed.

The religious vocation, then, is the vocation of a man who has become aware of the call and who, in an attitude of detached humility, responds to the call with total generosity. It is a vocation in the fullest sense of the word. It is not essentially a choice in the sense of a deliberation about a state of life. It is essentially rooted in a call. And it is God who calls. The call does not go out to all men, but those to whom it is directed bear the frightening responsibility which every man of God feels: "You have not chosen Me, but I have chosen you" (John 15:16).

God has laid His hands upon the religious man. The individual's awareness of personal vocation carries with it the knowledge that he has been summoned to a total dedication of his life to God. This knowledge may often be no more than an intimation. There may have been no sensible attraction, no "inspiration." But there is an unrest and a compelling urgency. The response must be given. At times there is distress, since the individual realizes that in this response lies the hazard of an entire life. There are necessarily moments of discomfort and uncertainty. Yet there can be no response without confidence in the grace of Him who calls. With the realization that one can rely upon grace, peace outweighs distress, joy overcomes discomfort. The dominant mood becomes one of confident love.

It is love that unites the whole of the religious man's actions. Love orientates man toward God and toward His will. Yet even this love originates in God. Even man's surrender of self to God is made possible by God's grace. All man must do is consent. And God so values this consent that He wishes man to renew it over and over again—with increasing understanding and with a constantly deepening love. This is what Guardini has called the seriousness of divine love—the paradoxical, humbling fact that God so values man's love that He places Himself to this extent at man's mercy.

Man's love, then, is a free love of his Creator. The perfection of love is proportioned to its generosity. St. Theresa of Lisieux wrote that nothing but the entire immolation of self can be called love. And Charles de Foucauld knew, in the instant when he knew there was a God, that he could do nothing other than live only for Him.

The whole purpose of religious life is to live only for God. Christian asceticism is the endeavor to attain Christian perfection, that perfection which consists simply in fulfilling as well as possible the will of God. The religious vocation is not, however, a call to merely personal salvation.

The man of God must be interested in social transformation, in the salvation of all men. Vocation is expansive—it involves oneself, other men, society, the world, history.

Yet the real starting point of the religious vocation is the individual. The religious man must find for himself the will of God. This is by no means easy. The ideal of personal holiness cannot be summarized in a plaster image or in a catalogue of the virtues. Authentic sanctity is personal, the responsibility of the person to his own personal truth.

All sanctity, if it is to be authentic, must be bound up with authentic human life—and hence with the uniqueness, the limited talents and potentialities, the emotional maturity of the individual.[8] The natural complements the supernatural. In this chapter the attempt has been made to sketch briefly the genesis of the religious vocation along its supernatural dimensions. Vocation here does not refer to the mere external process of entering the religious community. Rather vocation is taken in a broader sense, implying a call which invites a free and generous response. The call is our Lord's. The free response requires an initial attitude of detachment and humility and can only be made adequately by a fully mature, spiritually formed man.

But maturity in spiritual development ordinarily implies maturity at more basic natural and psychological levels. God's grace runs along channels of His own making. Generally He will follow the natural laws of human development as He interacts with man in the redemptive work. This is obvious in the case of the child. The child's spiritual activity is commensurate to his psychological aptitude. But the same is true of the adult. There are shadings and gradations in the psychological aptitude of physically mature

[8] Josef Goldbrunner, *Holiness Is Wholeness* (New York: Pantheon, 1955), p. 27.

individuals. And there are different stages in the emotional and psychological development of the adult person.

Although stages of psychological development may be logically and theoretically distinguished, they, like their counterparts in the process of supernatural development, typically tend to merge, and generally follow no rigid temporal sequence. Perhaps in a single instance the individual will pass swiftly through the various stages and attain relatively complete psychological maturity while still physically an adolescent. This is possible under certain circumstances, but normally the psychological growth process corresponds to the physical pattern. In this sense maturity is relative, and depends upon physical and chronological factors.

The following chapter outlines briefly the psychological growth process characteristic of childhood and adolescence, and provides a theoretical framework for discussion in subsequent chapters of the various stages of adult psychological development. Within such a framework it is perhaps possible to understand more fully how God's grace interacts with man's nature.

Psychological Development

2 One of the most significant of Sigmund Freud's contributions to modern psychology and psychiatry is the emphasis he placed on the importance of childhood experiences in later personality development and adjustment. Man is constantly molding his own fate, and no one of his actions is without significance for the future. The past is part of the man himself, and its events leave indelible marks on a man's character. Freud was convinced that childhood was the most important part of the past and that if painful conflicts are not adequately resolved in this period, they will continue to influence the individual's thoughts, feelings, and behavior—unconsciously causing emotional tension and inability to cope with the real world. The roots of adult emotional and psychological disorders Freud believed to lie basically in childhood experiences.

Many of Freud's insights have been debated by subsequent theorists in psychology and psychiatry, but rarely has his emphasis upon the importance of childhood been questioned. Nevertheless, Freudian theory of the psychology of the child has received considerable elaboration and modification in the hands of his successors. The most significant single contribution to this area has been the theory of "ego epigenesis" proposed by Erik H. Erikson.

Erikson's theory outlines a sequence of phases of personality development which spans an entire life cycle. This constitutes "ego epigenesis"—the developmental process whereby the central core of the personality—the ego—is structured. The process terminates in ego integrity or complete psychological maturity.

Erikson's sequence of the phases of personality development parallels the earlier Freudian conception of libido development—Freud's schema for the psychosexual development of the infant and the young child. However, Erikson's theory extends the original Freudian notions to the whole of the life process and hence is the first psychoanalytic theory to encompass those phases of the life cycle which are customarily subsumed under the single concept of adult maturity.

As a theory, Erikson's conceptualization of the developmental process is an abstraction derived from phenomenological and clinical sources of evidence. Consequently, the theory is "open" and subject to revision. Like any theory, its purpose is descriptive and explanatory. Further evidence may require radical changes on the descriptive level and new explanatory concepts. At best, the theory permits a greater understanding of the dynamic processes involved in human development. At worst, the theory abstracts from the reality and the complexity of life and fragmentizes the experienced totality. Hopefully, however, the advantages of the theory compensate for its disadvantages.

Any developmental sequence unfolds according to the laws of nature. In nature, all growing things follow specific patterns of development. Various parts are differentiated and hold ascendancy at certain phases of the sequence. In the end, all of the parts combine to produce the functioning whole. In the same fashion, the child at birth abandons the chemical environment of the womb and en-

ters the social environment of society. Here he meets the
opportunities and limitations of his culture. His gradually
increasing capacities—locomotor, sensory, social—develop
according to a prescribed sequence. The child learns to
crawl, stand, walk, to distinguish items in the environment,
to interact with other people.

On a more personal level, the child undergoes unique
inner experiences and conflicts. In this manner he develops
his own distinct personality complexus. Here, too, there are
patterns of development. These depend upon the social environment and to this extent vary from culture to culture.
Nevertheless, the growth of personality—like the growth of
the child's physical capacities—follows its own proper rate
and proper sequence. Personality develops along pre-
determined dimensions in accordance with the individual's
readiness to interact with a widening social environment,
beginning with the dim image of his mother and ending
with all mankind—or at least with that portion of mankind
with which the individual comes in contact during the
course of his lifetime.

In Erikson's formulation, these dimensions of growth
are divided into phases in the life sequence, each of which
is characterized by a specific developmental process. Because of intellectual or physical maturation, the person at
a given age confronts a new life task. A set of choices and
tests are determined for him by his society's structure. Each
of these life tasks involves a crisis. The resolution of this
crisis prepares the individual to face and resolve the subsequent crises of development. Failure to achieve a resolution
means impairment of the life cycle and the danger of failure
at subsequent levels of development.

Each crisis is a step taken in the direction of the next.
Each is a link in the chain of development. The solution
of any one crisis is prepared for in previous phases and

worked out to its completion only in subsequent ones.
Erikson has described these phases in terms of their ex-
tremes of successful and unsuccessful solution:

(1) basic trust versus mistrust
(2) autonomy versus shame and doubt
(3) initiative versus guilt
(4) industry versus inferiority
(5) identity versus identity diffusion
(6) intimacy versus isolation
(7) generativity versus stagnation
(8) integrity versus despair.[1]

In his book, *Identity and the Life Cycle*,[2] Erikson de-
lineates these phases and suggests how their resolution
contributes to healthy personality. Each crisis in the developmental sequence involves a change in perspective.
There must be a radical adjustment. The child, for example, fears being separated from his mother in one
phase of his development. At another point in development this fear has vanished and the child's greatest desire
is to be independent. He has faced the critical alternative
between being a dependent creature and an autonomous
one, and has resolved it in favor of autonomy. Each crisis
ideally terminates in such a new adjustment.

The first crisis is that of early infancy. What is at
stake here—in Erikson's terminology—is whether a man's
inner mood will be determined more by basic trust or
basic mistrust. Trust here connotes an adequate trustful-
ness in others and a simple sense of trustworthiness as far
as oneself is concerned. This trust is basic in the sense

[1] Erik H. Erikson, *Childhood and Society* (New York: Norton,
1950), pp. 219 ff.
[2] Erik H. Erikson, *Identity and the Life Cycle* (New York: International Univer. Press, 1959).

that it is a fundamental characteristic of personality, not a conscious habit, but an unconsciously assimilated attitude or orientation toward life.

The crisis typically occurs in the second part of the first year and has several aspects, corresponding temporally to three developments. First, there is a physiological stage in which general tension is associated with a violent drive to incorporate and appropriate. Second, there is a psychological stage during which the child becomes increasingly aware of himself as a distinct person. Finally, there is an environmental stage in which the mother apparently turns away from the infant toward other pursuits which had been abandoned during pregnancy and the early days of the child's postnatal life. It is against the combination of these impressions of having been deprived, of having been divided, and of having been abandoned—all of which engender a sense of basic mistrust—that basic trust must be established and maintained.

At this point in his development the child lives and loves with his mouth. Consequently, psychoanalytic theory has denominated this the "oral" phase of psychological development. The "oral character" of psychiatric literature is often characterized by depressive and pessimistic tendencies which can be traced to infantile mistrust and fears of being left alone or empty. This may produce, in turn, a cruel need to appropriate from others. But this stage of orality may also terminate in optimism and a fundamental trust.

The outcome of this crisis is largely determined by the quality of maternal care. The newborn infant's initial contact with the external world is with his mother and her desire and ability to feed and welcome him. The mother's attention and her gratification of the child's needs lend a certain predictability and hopefulness to an otherwise urgent and bewildering combination of external and internal stimuli.

It must be noted that the amount of the child's trust is not proportionate to the absolute quantity of food or demonstrations of love given him, but rather depends on the quality of the maternal relationship. Mothers instill a sense of trust in their children by a sensitive care of the child's individual needs and a firm sense of personal trustworthiness. Parents guide their children not merely by the prohibitions and permissions they administer; they must also attempt to inculcate within the child a deep, almost somatic conviction that there is meaning in what they are doing. This demands that they act on principle and from motives of love, not out of anger or hostile and selfish resentment. If there is love and if the parents believe in the meaning of the principles which motivate them, then the child will come to believe in his parents and to see them as trustworthy.

In a sense, basic trust is closely related to religion. The parent who possesses a lively sense of faith and deep religious convictions reinforces the child's basic trust in the world's trustworthiness. Erikson feels that for centuries religious faith has inculcated this sense of trust and given tangible form to a sense of evil. Religion encourages a childlike surrender to God and His divine Providence. Man's sense of intrinsic dependence upon God, his prayer and worship, his need for grace—these stimulate faith and provide solid foundations for trust. Grounded in his own faith, the parent's sense of trust is transmitted to the child—imperceptibly, almost unconsciously—in the form of basic trust.

The second crisis of childhood, usually resolved by the fourth year, develops the child's sources of the sense of autonomy. The child learns, literally, to stand on his own two feet. He develops an autonomy and the ability to perform certain tasks independently of others. He may, however, develop a strong willfulness and perhaps hostility. This stage is decisive for the ratio between cooperation and willfulness, love and hate, that will characterize his later life. From self-control the child gains a lasting sense of autonomy and freedom of self-expression. On the other hand, a loss of self-control and parental overcontrol result in a lasting sense of doubt and shame.

The child during this period comes to delineate between the world of "I" and "mine" and "you" and "yours." He will cling to his own possessions and then discard them. This ambiguity follows from muscular maturation which allows experimentation with two simultaneous sets of social modalities—holding on and letting go. The child experiences basic conflicts which lead ultimately to either hostile or benign expectations and attitudes. "To hold" may become synonymous with a destructive and cruel retaining or it may provide the basis for adult care and concern. "To let go" can turn into a hostile letting loose of destructive forces or it may give rise to a healthy attitude of resignation, letting pass the misfortunes of life without undue grief and emotional distress. The alternative again depends to a great extent upon the character of parental training.

The child whose parents are firm and yet tolerant learns to be firm and tolerant with himself. He develops his sense of pride and autonomy; he grants autonomy to others. Firmness protects him against the potential anarchy of his newly discovered capacity to choose and to appropriate, to hold on and to let go. Yet a tolerant environment must also support his wish to be independent, to stand on his own feet. If this is not granted, the child may be overcome by a sense of having exposed himself prematurely and foolishly, by a sense of shame and doubt.

This stage has been called the beginning of moral responsibility and the dawn of conscience.[3] During the first few years of life the parents best serve the child and help him to gain a sense of trust by satisfying his needs with meaningful and sincerely felt love and affection. During the next few years parents must help the child achieve his sense of autonomy by a careful cooperation with maturation and by firmness and tolerance. The period of autonomy training is of special importance because it is the time when the child begins in earnest his lifelong learning process. Parental prohibition or permission during this critical initial period tends to instill semi-permanent or permanent modifications of behavior. These are not, of course, rationally formed habits. They are rather automatisms which provide the necessary basis for the development at a later stage of habits of virtue. Hence the beginnings of concience are formed at this stage at an essentially non-rational, emotional level. This is the development of what the psychologist calls the "superego," the emotional foundation of the rational conscience. Once the child comes to use his own reasoning powers, he may internalize old values or exchange them for new ones—though these rational processes may be greatly inhibited by earlier emotional learning.

This stage of autonomy, then, is the stage at which the child is taught his first values. There are many psychologists who would maintain that later sanctity is greatly conditioned by automatisms developed during these early years. Certainly the process may be greatly facilitated or greatly retarded by the events of these years. The child's attitude

[3] Robert J. Havighurst, *Human Development and Education* (New York: Longmans, Green, 1953), pp. 19–20. The discussion of the moral development of the child in this chapter largely follows the lines of thought originally suggested by Ned H. Cassem, S.J., "The Moral Development of Children," an unpublished manuscript, St. Louis University, 1959.

toward the content of Christian morality is inculcated at
this time. The parent transmits to the child his own values,
his own attitude to the essential questions of life. If the
parent wishes the child to see in Christianity a true and
deeply meaningful answer to these questions, he must himself be convinced of its truth and meaningfulness. The child
may later reject the values his parents teach him at this
time, but these values have been embedded deeply in an
emotional and essentially non-rational stratum of his personality and are later modified only with great difficulty.

Once he has determined that he is an autonomous person,
the child endeavors to ascertain what kind of person he is
to be. This precipitates the third crisis of the developmental cycle. The child wants, above all, to be like his
parents, who appear to him very powerful. Three developments help at this stage, augmenting his aspiration to
identify with his parents. First, the child learns to move
around more freely and more easily, and establishes a wider
and seemingly unlimited radius of goals. Second, his
ability to communicate with persons in his environment
increases, enabling him to understand and misunderstand
their intentions in his regard. Finally, increased facility in
locomotion and language permits him to expand his
imagination, increasing the rôle fantasy and autistic thinking play in his life. Out of all this there must emerge a
sense of unbroken initiative as the basis for realistic ambition and independence.

This third crisis of the developmental cycle involves what
Freud described as the central complex of the family—the
Oedipus complex. It corresponds to the Freudian phallic
stage of psychosexuality. According to Erikson, this crisis
centers in the unconscious association of sensual freedom
with the body of the mother, the association of cruel in-

hibition with the interference of the father, and consequent love and hatred in reality and fantasy. Although such a theory offends certain sensitivities, it has strong clinical support. There is a reluctance to associate childhood with hatred and destructiveness, but though an age without guilt, childhood is not an age without evil. It is illogical to assume that hatred and envy introduce themselves only when the person has attained the full use of his reason. Moreover, the sexual aspects of this stage are well documented, supporting the contention that human beings pass through two puberties, an abortive one and a proper one.

During this period the child's initiative develops. It is a time of intense reality testing and imitation of adult behavior. Contact with reality requires that the child repress or forget many of his fondest hopes. His newly developed imagination is gradually tamed, and he learns necessary self-restraint—even interest in such impersonal things as the three R's.

The supergo becomes fully developed during this period. The child feels shame and fear. He even feels guilt for thoughts and deeds that no one else witnessed. It is important to note that the supergo is essentially irrational. It is primitive, cruel, and uncompromising. It often drives the child to an obedience that is more literal than the one the parents wish to exact. It can constrict the child to the point of total inhibition, and foster deep resentment when parents are seen as not living up to the ideals and duties which they have imposed upon the child. One of the most severe conflicts in life involves hatred for a parent who served as the model of the superego, but who was found guilty of transgressions the child can no longer tolerate in himself. Such a child may come in later life to view morality as a matter of vindictiveness and the suppression of others.

Such rigid adult moralism (which is not to be confused

with morality) is the residual of the child's moralism at
this earlier stage of his development. The consequences of
the guilt aroused at this stage often do not appear until
much later, when conflicts over initiative may result in a
self-restriction which keeps the individual from living up to
his capacities. There may, on the other hand, be a com-
pensatory over-initiative, a tireless zest for activity. Many
adults feel that their worth as persons consists entirely in
doing something, rather than in being someone. The strain
they consequently develop in their bodies, even at moments
of rest, plays an important part in the formation of a frequent type of contemporary pathology—psychosomatic
disease.

Such pathology is symptomatic of the neglect of valuable
human resources, a neglect initiated in childhood. The
problem, Erikson feels, is one of mutual regulation. When
the child, passing through this stage of overly rigid moralism, is allowed to gradually develop a sense of responsibility,
to gain some feeling for the institutions, functions, and
rôles which permit him to anticipate his responsibility as
an adult participant in society, he becomes capable of
pleasurable accomplishment—particularly in meaningful
play and in taking care of himself and younger children.
He becomes eager and able to interact socially in construct-
ing and planning.

Such a successful resolution depends to a large extent
upon the character of parental discipline. It is through
discipline that the child's need for initiative is channeled
along constructive lines. However, psychologists caution
that discipline should be administered consistently and per-
tinently, so that the child knows that the punishment
applies to this particular activity (not to him). There
should be outlets for the child's desires, yet discipline

should be realistic and allow the child to experience some of the sting of reality. Few rules should be demanded of the child, and, in general, disciplinary measures should follow maturation. Any discipline, however, must be administered with affection, without indignation, anger, or impatience.[4] In its most general sense, discipline is simply the definition of the environment in which the child is permitted to carry on his activities, and as such should always be an environment pervaded by love and affection.

Above all, parental discipline must be supplemented by parental example. The child cannot be expected to reject flesh and blood for a moral abstraction. Discrepancy between parental words and actions is the most insurmountable barrier the child faces in the development of his moral convictions. Possibly such discrepant behavior on the part of an adult can mar the child's attitude for life. This possibility should make any parent (or teacher) uneasy. If discipline is to be at all effective, it must be reinforced by behavior. To teach a child a value, to bring him to accept a system of religious ideals and beliefs, it is necessary first of all that the one teaching hold this value, these ideals and beliefs, with conviction. Otherwise no amount of discipline will convince the child.

If it is administered properly and supplemented by good example, discipline will fulfill definite needs of the child. Psychologists have pointed out that a child will tend to interpret a wholly permissive attitude as indifference. Discipline brings a sense of security, lessens the weight of guilt, and provides opportunity for praise and motivation. The child is taught a reasonable degree of conformity and the important lesson that the world responds in an orderly and

[4] Joseph L. Stone and Joseph Church, *Childhood and Adolescence* (New York: Random House, 1957), pp. 133–135.

consistent fashion to his actions. But even more importantly, discipline helps the child develop self-control and self-direction.[5]

The healthy outgrowth of proper discipline should be the transformation of hatred and destructiveness into an identification with parental-figures and with parents themselves. Realistic identification is based upon an experience of essential equality in worth, in spite of inequality in strength and age. Such equality provides the basis for early prevention of fear and guilt and facilitates free interpersonal collaboration. This permits a free sense of enterprise and the peaceful cultivation of initiative.

If such a sense of equality is lacking and parental discipline is overly strict, the child internalizes a threatening superego and rigid, exaggerated ethical attitudes. The result is self-restriction or over-compensation and the danger of pathology.

In the fourth developmental stage, the child—now between six and eleven years old—must achieve a sense of industry. Frequently the trend begins earlier as the child becomes capable of learning systematically and collaborating with others. But now he is in the period of formal schooling. Between childhood and adulthood the individual goes to school—to a school that seems to be a world all by itself, with its own goals and limitations, its achievements and disappointments. It is here that a sense of industry develops, a sense of pleasure in work completed through steady attention and persevering diligence.

Healthy resolution of the dangers inherent in this stage of development leads to a sense of duty and accomplishment. The child lays aside fantasy and play for the under-

[5] Elizabeth B. Hurlock, *Child Development* (New York: McGraw-Hill, 1956), pp. 420–423.

taking of real tasks and the development of academic and social competence. Failure to achieve a successful resolution results in a feeling of inadequacy and inferiority. This may be precipitated by an insufficient solution of the preceding conflict—the child may still prefer to be the baby at home rather than the student at school. Or he may suffer in comparing himself to his father, failing to effect an identification founded on equality of worth.

If this identification does take place, this period is characterized by a conscious imitation of parental values and rôles. The child's behavior is no longer merely a complexus of automatisms. It is now rational and deliberate. Although his judgment is still poor and his powers of abstraction are still limited, he is capable of understanding why certain things are done or not done, and can apply a common principle to a variety of situations. Consequently, parents must teach him the bases beneath his customs and automatisms— though still with reference to the concrete after-effects of his actions on himself and others. This conscious identification with parental values develops the child's self-ideal, and thereby counteracts the depersonalizing influence of the peer group which the child at this time is beginning to experience.

It should be noted that in Erikson's formulation this period of a developing sense of industry does not involve a crisis originating in the inventory of basic human drives. Rather it is a case of outer hindrances to development. This stage differs from the others in that it is not marked by a swing from violent inner upheaval to new mastery. The reason why Freud called this the latency period is that violent drives are typically dormant at this time. This period is in this sense the lull before the storm of puberty.

Yet this stage is socially most decisive. The child learns to work in conjunction with others. A sense of division of

labor and equality of opportunity develops at this time. If
the child comes to feel that the color of his skin, the background of his parents, or the cost of his clothes will decide
his social worth, lasting harm may ensue to his sense of
identity.

The crisis of identity is the crisis of adolescence. The
adolescent seeks to clarify his understanding of who he is
and what his rôle is to be. He hopes to forge for himself a
perspective and direction, to achieve an effective integration out of the remnants of his childhood and the hopes of
his anticipated adulthood. Failure to resolve this crisis can
result in neurosis, psychosis, or delinquent behavior. More
frequently, however, there is a generalized sense of rôle
diffusion.

In some young people, in some classes, at certain periods
of history, the identity crisis is minimal. In other people,
classes, and periods, this crisis is clearly marked off as a
critical period. There is considerable evidence to suggest
that in contemporary American culture the identity crisis is
of maximal importance. The American man feels a desperate urgency—often concealed under the camouflage of
social conventions—to resolve the problem of what he is to
believe in and who he is to be or become.

Consequently, the problem of identity is not merely a
problem of adolescence. In our culture it is a problem
which spans adolescence and is usually not resolved until
adulthood, if ever. In this connection, Erikson distinguishes
between the identity crisis and identity formation. Identity
formation is a lifelong process. The identity crisis, however, does typically occur at the end of adolescence. But
since a number of forces working in combination have extended the period of adolescence, since modern young
people undergo a prolonged adolescence, the individual

may not experience this identity crisis until his twenty-fifth or even thirtieth year. For this reason the problem of identity will be dealt with separately, as a problem of young adulthood, in a later chapter.

Three crises—those of adulthood—follow the crisis of identity. They concern problems of intimacy, generativity, and integrity. What rôle diffusion is to identity—its alternative and danger—isolation is to intimacy, egocentric non-productivity is to generativity, and the lack of consistent values is to integrity. When the identity crisis is prolonged, these three crises are interwoven with it, and the resolution of the identity crisis may occur at a point temporally simultaneous with one or all of these crises. Whatever the case, a lasting sense of ego identity is a necessary ingredient in the mature personality.

A discussion of these problems of adulthood may be profitably reserved for later chapters; at this point it is helpful to mention some of the problems facing the adolescent. For adolescence is to some extent always with us, and its residuals are especially prominent in the young adult. The scars of one's adolescence do not heal overnight. And in keeping with the purpose of this book, special attention will be paid here to the moral and religious development of the adolescent.

Basic to the adolescent's struggle for identity is his need for a philosophy of life. He is not old enough or experienced enough to formulate a coherent philosophy, but he feels compelled to make a beginning. This need becomes more intense under the conditions of a rapidly changing society where many parents find it difficult to resolve conflicting values. The mass media of communication add to the confusion, since everyone's ideas are made available to everyone else through these media, but integration is left to the consumer. These create for the adolescent discordant and seemingly irresolvable value-tensions.

But there are other sources of tension as well. The anthropologist Ruth Benedict has proposed her theory of "cultural discontinuities"[6] to provide a possible explanation for the origin of some of the central conflicts of the adolescent period. The theory emphasizes the sharp discontinuity American culture establishes in the developmental process from childhood to adulthood. In general, the theory states that our society demands that children be taught certain patterns of behavior which must be discarded later if the individual is to be a successful adult. Children, for example, are expected to be irresponsible. They make no labor contribution to the industrial society. Yet as adults they are expected to assume the responsibility of earning a living and keeping a home. In other societies this discrepancy is not present—there is continuous training for a responsible rôle. At an early age children participate with adults in performing tasks which are essential to the community.

There is a similar discontinuity in our culture with respect to dominant and submissive behavior. Children are expected to obey adults, until the time when they too as adults are required to assume the rôle of dominance. Again, such a pattern of behavior contrasts with that of simpler societies where it is expected that a child who is docile or dominant will be accordingly a docile or dominant adult.

There is also a discontinuity in the sexual rôle expected of the child and the adult. The child in our society is expected to be sexless until he is physically mature. The adult must accept his sex rôle. There is a strong resistance to the

[6] "Continuities and Discontinuities in Cultural Conditioning," *Psychiatry*, 1 (1938), 161–167.

notion of childhood sexuality in our culture—a resistance which is based on an essentially un-Christian doctrine which associates sex with wickedness. Consequently, the adolescent frequently finds it extremely difficult to disassociate sex and evil.

The personality may be severely affected by such discontinuities. The developmental process may become clogged. The result is consequent regression and lasting emotional distortions. The child that once was tends to reappear from time to time with childish solutions to the problems of daily life. The individual is emotionally immature.

Typically, however, there is a generalized state of rebellion. This is the product of the adolescent's desire to resolve discontinuties and to find a personally authentic philosophy of life, combined with a rigid and extreme idealism. In rebellion he lashes out at the falseness of the world and challenges existing values—his parents' especially and his own. He seeks and settles upon over-simplified and over-idealized solutions which are generally impractical and rarely held for any length of time.

The adolescent's spirit of rebellion and his idealism can provide the basis for solid moral development. During this stage the adolescent is greatly influenced by reflective and logical arguments. Since no moral act is virtuous unless it is a rational act, adolescence is the period which determines whether the sentient and emotional foundations laid in childhood will terminate in real virtue. This is why adolescent rebellion is an advantage. His spirit of rebellion can be profitably exploited to bring him to question every custom, value, and convention that has previously been taken for granted. If he can be given insight, rationally and logically through instruction and information, into the reasonableness of his values and the irrationality of their op-

posites, he will achieve solid, independent moral values of
his own—values that are human and personally meaningful
because they are fundamentally rational. Adolescent idealism aids in this process, giving the individual something
to rebel for and making it possible for him to accept lofty
and challenging moral values.

Religious values, however, seem to have little importance
for most adolescents. Contrary to the widespread belief
there is no rampant repudiation of religion during adolescence. Most adolescents attend church regularly, rely on
prayer, and believe in a personal God. Yet studies show
that young people typically find religion an amorphous
body of beliefs symbolized by meaningless words. The
import of religious teaching is unclear; its bearing on their
personal lives is not perceived; and very few adolescents
seem to be able to integrate the values of religion into the
pattern of everyday life. Religion is little more than a
vague set of explanations and terms which are accepted
as true and valid, but which have little operational rele-
vance to the person's value system.

In the development of religious values, as in the development of moral values, the young person's convictions and
attitudes are of necessity built upon what has been previously learned and accepted. The individual's upbringing
and his total personality development until the time of
adolescence will have a significant bearing on his religious
orientation during adolescent years. For religious faith and
religious devotion consist in a close and intimate association with the Person of an infinite and all-loving God. The
relationship between the believer and his God is one which
involves the whole being, body and soul, of the religious
man. Religion is not meant to supply the neurotic with a
means of escaping the pressures of reality. The religious

person must be capable of bringing his whole self before God—and the whole self includes the past.

Like the child, the adolescent's attitude toward religion is greatly determined by the attitude of those around him. The adolescent will find it difficult to accept creeds and doctrines inculcating faith, hope, and charity, if he has had no past experience with believing, trusting, and loving people. He will look to the lives of those who teach him religious beliefs to see how belief and trust and love are manifested. If there is a marked dichotomy between what is taught and what is practiced, the adolescent may ultimately reject religious ideals and beliefs altogether.

However, general increase in religious skepticism does not occur in adolescence. There is less acceptance of more literal, ritualistic, and dogmatic aspects of religious belief. As a result of intellectual maturation, religious beliefs become more abstract and less literal. God becomes conceptualized—He is an omniscient power rather than an old man with a beard. But studies by social psychologists show that there is relatively little basic change in religious belief, even during the college years. Atheism is an extremely rare outcome of college education.

Nevertheless, the findings of such studies are deceptive. There is considerable reason to believe that, although there is no overt repudiation, young people show resistance to the idea of self-examination in the area of religious values. This contrasts sharply with the adolescent's attitudes regarding other values, and suggests that little thought is given to religious values. Religion is for many young people an empty convention, a superstition or vague magic which keeps off misfortune, a type of insurance policy. There are frequently no intellectual convictions concerning religious beliefs and no desire to inquire into one's beliefs.

There are possibly unconscious reasons for this fear of examining one's personal religious values. Doubts about religion and religious belief have a serious emotional impact upon the young person. To question religious belief is to question the very image of God upon which he has built his faith and which has become his ultimate basis for truth. The adolescent, consequently, becomes uncomfortable when he doubts. He feels that he should establish his own religious convictions, but he is unconsciously fearful that any questioning will take from his life all truth and meaning. He desires the independence that will follow from personal consideration of religious beliefs, but he unconsciously hesitates before such radical and final independence and therefore avoids serious reflection on so fundamental a level.

Yet if his religious convictions are to be mature and intelligent, there must be a critical self-examination. Such self-examination is necessary for healthy growth. It is probably true that the more certain the adolescent becomes about his religious convictions, the freer he will feel to test them. The more they mean to him, the more he will have the courage to question them. The adolescent who is most capable of believing is also the one who dares to doubt.[7]

In summary, religious development parallels psychological development. Every child is a potential saint. Yet his capacity for sanctity is to a great extent dependent upon forces external to the self. Above all, the child's parents determine the environment in which he is to grow and develop physically, psychologically, and spiritually. Where there is an atmosphere of love and affection, where the child is respected as a person, a son of God through grace,

[7] Arthur T. Jersild, *The Psychology of Adolescence* (New York: Macmillan, 1957), p. 337.

the normal outcome of this development will be a healthy sense of trust, a sense of autonomy, of initiative, and of industry. And where there is an atmosphere of faith, a firm conviction and belief in spiritual reality, the child will assimilate the attitude of faith—unconsciously perhaps, and at an essentially non-rational level—as the foundation for his own mature religious convictions.

In adolescence the religious beliefs of childhood must be questioned and established rationally and intellectually. Typically, this is a task many adolescents would rather avoid. Often there is an outward indifference to religion, perhaps an unconscious fear of doubting religious values which have considerable emotional significance in the individual's life. But unless these religious beliefs are established rationally, there can be no progress in spiritual development. If it is not founded upon solid intellectual convictions, the young person's religion is basically an unhealthy and childish emotionalism. The individual remains spiritually immature.

As in moral development, the adolescent's spirit of rebellion and his idealism can play important rôles in spiritual formation. His rebellion can be employed to lead him to challenge his values and beliefs and ultimately to give intellectual assent to those he accepts. His idealism makes it possible for him to aspire to the most difficult of all goals —that of the perfection of Christian living. And Christian education should be the soil in which such intellectual convictions develop, where young people encounter the highest spiritual ideals. This is the soil of the religious vocation.

Identity

3 In a sense adolescence is part of childhood and part of adulthood. The child at different stages of his development identifies with those particular aspects of people by which he is most immediately affected. These aspects are not necessarily favored for their social acceptability, but rather because of the nature of the child's fantasy and his immature and unrealistic wishes. By the end of adolescence these identifications have merged and become subordinated to a single identity which includes all significant past identifications, but which also alters them to make a unique and reasonably coherent whole. Adolescent identity in its final development lacks the playfulness of infancy and the boundless zest of childhood. There is a seriousness, an adult sense of purpose and dedication.

Cultural forces interact to bring the adolescent to choose and decide once and for all what his own identity is to be. The task society imposes is formidable. It necessitates in our culture a long intermediate period of preparation. Erikson refers to such a period as a psychosocial moratorium[1] during which the individual goes to school to learn

[1] Erik H. Erikson, *Identity and the Life Cycle* (New York: International University Press, 1959), p. 111. The author wishes to express his gratitude to the Editor of the *Review for Religious* for allowing him to reprint in this chapter certain material which first appeared in that publication.

42

the technical and social requirements necessary for the professional situation to which he eventually will commit himself. The young person experiments during this time with various professional rôles until he finds the one to which he seems suited. In finding it, he gains an assured sense of inner identity and continuity. Consequently, he is able to bridge what he was as a child and what he is about to become, to reconcile his conception of himself and society's recognition of him.

This period of psychosocial moratorium is necessarily prolonged in our society because of the complexity of modern living and the subsequent need for extensive technological training. Therefore, adolescence itself is prolonged and with it the adolescent's crisis of identity. The crisis of identity is finally resolved, not by the child that was, but by the adult that is to be.

While the identity crisis is the particular problem of the young adult, its roots lie deeper—in a lifelong development which Erikson calls the process of identity formation. These roots extend to the first instance of self-recognition— to the infant's earliest exchange of smiles, which couples a sense of self-realization with a mutual recognition. All through childhood this sense of selfhood develops. But it is dangerously threatened during adolescence.

The discontinuities of psychosocial development which are felt in their intensity during this period of adolescence lead to a lack of self-certainty. The individual is puzzled and may wonder why, for example, he was first made to believe that it is admirable to be "little," only to be forced to exchange this status for a new one and to accept the consequences and duties of being "big." Such discontinuities exaggerate the incipient crisis, bringing it quickly to a head. But no immediate solution is to be found. The individual commences his psychosocial moratorium. Only gradually

does his sense of identity develop. For many of our contemporaries the problem is never resolved.

Victor Frankl, one of the leading proponents of existential psychology, has pointed out that Freudian psychoanalysis has introduced into psychological theory what it
calls the pleasure principle or the will-to-pleasure. Adler
has made psychologists conversant with the rôle of the will-
to-power as a main factor in the formation of neurosis. But
Frankl maintains that man is dominated neither by the
will-to-pleasure nor by the will-to-power, but by what he
would call man's will-to-meaning, that is, man's deep-seated
striving for a higher and ultimate meaning to his existence.[2]
Frankl has perhaps overstated his case. It is more likely
a question of emphasis. But the will-to-meaning does reflect
the modern concern with personal identity and, in this
sense, is probably as strategic in our time as the study of
sexuality was in Freud's time or the study of the drive for
power in Adler's time.

For many of our contemporaries the normal condition of
human life is sorrow. It is a sorrow concerned with social
and economic conditions, but rooted more basically in the
undeniably crucial question: whether man can be himself.
Stated more radically, it is the question the French author
Camus raised: whether life is worth living or not, whether
it has meaning or not. Is man his own master, free and possessing the dignity and love to be true to himself and joy-
ous? In many cases there is a pessimistic conviction that the
modern world has so mastered man and depersonalized
him that, as Camus wrote, there is only one remaining
philosophical question under the conditions of modern
life—that of suicide.

[2] Victor Frankl, *From Death Camp to Existentialism* (Boston:
Beacon Press, 1959), p. 97.

Tolstoy once said that his life had taught him one truth—the truth that man's situation is desperate. When man has climbed to the highest level of his development, he sees at once that everything is falsehood and deception. This is the basis of his pessimism. It is a pessimism discovered by life—by the dark, primeval, and pervasive melody of earth-bound life. This is the pessimism prophetically felt by George Bernard Shaw when he realized that the science in which he had pinned his faith was bankrupt. He died the tragic death of an atheist who had lost his faith.

But the pessimism of life is most apparent in our own times and in our own country. It is seen, for example, in Arthur Miller's play, *Death of a Salesman,* in the character Biff Loman. Biff has wandered from job to job, seeking the key to success in life. Finally he found it: it was to get on a hot subway on a hot morning in the summer, to devote one's whole life to keeping stock, making phone calls, or selling and buying, to suffer fifty weeks of the year for a two-week vacation, to always stay one step ahead of the other fellow. This was all that life had to offer Biff—and all it offers millions of Americans.

Psychologists and psychoanalysts have long recognized that patients and parents of prospective patients come to psychoanalysis hoping to find in the system a refuge from the depersonalization inherent in modern life and a key to the meaning of life. Perhaps the modern neurosis is best characterized by a syndrome which includes the conviction that existence is meaningless, a pessimism which is almost despair, and a loss of personal identity. In short, the modern neurosis is merely the expression of a prolonged identity crisis that has never been resolved.

To understand the etiology of this particular neurotic formation, it is perhaps helpful to consider several themes which have recurred in the writings of cultural critics. Depreciation of the American way of life is, of course, a favorite indoor sport. The pertinence of the critics' remarks is not always apparent, yet in the present context certain criticisms are relevant. They point out some of the reasons for the identity crises of contemporary Americans. From these criticisms some light may be thrown on the identity crisis of the American man and consequently on the identity crisis of the (American) religious man.

Arthur Miller's Biff exemplifies an American type. Society has failed to provide him with a clearly defined rôle: "I just can't take hold, Mom, I just can't take hold of some kind of life." He lives in constant frustration, unaware of who he is or what he is to be. And many psychoanalysts feel that Biff's number is legion.

That Biff should address his problems to Mom is significant. During World War II the expression "Momism" came into existence as a means of denoting a type of personality commonly encountered in young men. There is an excessive dependence upon and attachment to the mother, with but feeble attachment to the father and no clear image gained through him of man's rôle. Psychologists have commented upon the probable roots of this phenomenon: the absence, both physically and psychologically, of the father from many American urban and suburban homes. Because of the conditions of economic and social life, many fathers have neither the opportunity nor the inclination to "take on" their sons in the way that was common in the days of the older patriarchal society. This is the first cause that may be mentioned for the prolongation of the crisis of identity: the failure of the father in our culture to give to the son a clear image of the masculine personality and the rôle of man.

Critics have also noted the American fear of loneliness.

Individual identity is sacrificed in an effort to stay close to the herd, to be no different from others in thought, feeling, or action. To stand aside, to be alone, is to assert a personal identity which refuses to be submerged. Society will not tolerate this. Innumerable social features are designed to prevent it: stadiums to accommodate thousands at sport events, open doors of private rooms and offices, club cars on trains, shared room in colleges and boarding houses, countless clubs, organizations, associations, societies, canned music (for silence is unbearable) piped into hospitals, railway cars, and supermarkets.

Yet one of the surest signs of the resolution of the identity crisis is an increased capacity for being alone, for being responsible for oneself. The gradual process that will end in perfect identity involves an awareness of the fact that there are decisions in life and aspects of life's struggle that a person must face alone.

For as a young person becomes clearer in his own mind of his rôle in society and of his personal identity, he is likely also to become more aware of how he differs from others. Gradually he becomes conscious of his isolation from others, not because others are pulling away, but because the fullness of personal identity cannot be achieved without some degree of aloneness. Here there is a paradox: the more richly a person lives, the more lonely, in a sense, he becomes. And as a person, in this formative isolation, becomes more able to appreciate the moods and feelings of others, he also becomes more able to have meaningful relationships with them.

But the unwritten code of our national culture prohibits aloneness, and this is the second causative factor for a prolonged identity crisis: the obstacles our society imposes to prevent personal reflection.

Finally, the critics refer to the depersonalization of man

effected by the mass media. Man is losing himself to the
products of his own making. Much could be said about the
impact of the mass media upon man and especially of their
deleterious effects upon a sense of individual identity, but
much has already been said by the critics. What is of primary interest here is that mass media standardize thought
by supplying the spectator with a ready-made visual image
before he has had time to construct a rational interpreta-
tion of his own. Man has come to accept ideas and attitudes
without having submitted these to himself for intellectual
decision. Man is so much a part of the verbal noise going
on around him that he does not notice what the noise is
conveying to him.

There are, of course, many other causative factors con-
tributing to our national and individual identity crises.
Some of these have been mentioned previously. Yet millions
of young people face these and other psychological and
social obstacles to identity and transcend them in one way
or another. If not, they live, as Captain Ahab says, with
half their heart and with only one of their lungs, and the
world is the worse for it.

The religious man—the man who possesses a fundamentally God-oriented personality—is not, of course, immune
from cultural influences. Yet, as Erikson has observed in his
book on Luther, he is always older or suddenly becomes
older than his fellows and, in this sense, older than his
parents and teachers. He focuses in a precocious way on
what it usually takes others a lifetime to gain an inkling of:
the question of how to escape corruption in living and how
to give meaning to life in death. Because he experiences
such a breakthrough to the last problems so early in his
life, it is perhaps better for him to seal his message in a
young martyrdom or to become a hermit in a solitude

which anticipates eternity. We know little of Christ as a young man, but it is almost impossible to imagine him as middle-aged.[3]

This short cut between the youthful crisis of identity and the mature one of integrity constitutes the essence of the religious experience spoken of earlier. It is an intuition that conveys with it a sense of urgency—an urgency in some way similar to that which characterizes the intuition of the artist. But it need not be a dramatic or sudden intuition. Typically, there is an experienced need for generosity or the realization that a certain path leads to mediocrity. The decision is made to respond to the call.

If the individual is consistent in his generosity, he eventually must grapple with the acute and hazardous difficulties connected with religious transformation. The method of "indoctrination" to which he subjects himself aims at systematically descending to the frontiers where all ego dangers must be faced in the raw, where personal guilt is uncovered, drives tamed by prayer and asceticism, and where, ultimately, self must abandon and transform its own identity. In a certain sense, only "religious geniuses"[4] are capable of such an enterprise. Yet the man or woman who enters religious life specifically chooses to face this challenge. Perhaps the most important ramification of the life of the vows is the consequent necessity of mature personal identity.

Such a sense of identity presupposes secure emotional and psychological foundations. The individual must be capable of using and enjoying his emotional resources. Stated concretely, he must be able to derive satisfaction

[3] Erik H. Erikson, *Young Man Luther* (New York: Norton, 1958), p. 261.

[4] Jean Danielou, S.J., *God and the Ways of Knowing* (New York: Meridan, 1957), p. 10.

from pleasant things, to love and to laugh, to experience
anger when faced with injustice, to accept his fear without
false show of courage when faced with frightening things,
to go out to life, even though doing so means risking failure. In short, the young person must be mature before his
time in the sense that he has undergone a process of development which began in infancy, continued into adolescence, and revealed itself with increasing richness and an
increasing sense of identity as he moves into adulthood. At
length, hopefully, the person establishes his capacity for
relating himself to other persons in such a way that their
satisfaction becomes as important as his own. This is the
fundamental attitude of the religious man because it is the
beginning of Christianity—to love one's neighbor as oneself.

There are those, however, who consider such maturity
impossible in a young person. They regard it as dangerous,
unreasonable, and even in a sense against nature, to commit a young person in perpetuity to the religious life.
Martin Luther became convinced that religious commitment was out of the question for a man under thirty years
of age. A young man of twenty, he felt, does not know what
the future may have in store, what sacrifices he may have
to accept. He has only a very general view of what religious
life will be, and his final renunciation can only be made
when he knows in detail and as a whole what such a life
entails. Yet St. Thomas held that a person could decide
upon a religious vocation before puberty.

This poses a problem which involves more than a question of the religious vocation. It is concerned with one of
the fundamental aspects of the problem of life. The mature man is future-oriented; for him life is a continuous
whole. In his youth he finds that he must commit himself
to an identity, to a course to which he will remain bound

in the future. His acts are weighted with the future. If a man refuses to commit himself, identity becomes impossible.

Marriage and the religious vocation are the two fundamental forms of commitment. When a man marries, he is unaware of the trials and responsibilities of marriage. He does not know what it is to have a dependent wife and children. But the will to do that which is irrevocable depends on the strength of a person's love. A love which is genuine takes possession of the whole of the personality. Then it desires to be irrevocable.

Commitment involves the whole of oneself. It cannot be repudiated without repudiating something of the self. It is a commitment to the truth of one's life—and therefore to Truth, to God. Man stands in God's presence and, through an act which is ultimately an act of faith, commits himself to his own truth. There may be repudiation, but this is only to be understood as a fall.[5]

Such a notion of personal commitment leaves little room for the so-called "temporary vocation" (which is actually a contradiction in terms), even when this is understood as an act of the permissive will of God which allows a person, for his sanctification, to live for some time as a religious and with religious vows. Although a person does grow and develop as he lives out his commitment, although his initial love deepens into a more perfect and more mature love, there can be no possibility of a repudiation. This would be a denial of identity and is only explained by a "fall." These words are not, of course, meant to be dogmatic. The nature and binding force of a religious commitment such as life with vows requires much more adequate theological analysis.

[5] Gabriel Marcel, *Being and Having* (Glasgow: University Press, 1949), pp. 45–46.

Yet the problem remains. The religious man must establish his identity. Basically, it is a question of the acquisition of what Lindworsky calls the "vocational ideal."[6] Every man embodies a thought in the mind of God. All of his life is a struggle to measure up to the divine expectation. Only the saints approach the completion of God's desires. Yet the man of God must be constantly striving to achieve his personal ideal. His life represents, ultimately, a unique extension of Christ's life that must be manifested to the world.

This ideal represents a focal point for personal identity within the religious vocation. Perfect identity is not something acquired in its fullness all at once. It comes as the termination to a long and gradual process of growth. Each step along the way presents new difficulties and necessitates closer scrutiny and deeper meditation upon the nature of the identity chosen. There must be a gradual transformation and identification with Christ.

The vocational ideal guides the individual to his new identity within the confines of a life of the vows. Gradually the significance of each vow becomes apparent. Each involves a secondary crisis of its own, a danger to personal identity. Once each of these crises is faced and resolved, perfect identity is realized.

By his vow of poverty the religious man is thrust once more—this time on a much more conscious and more spiritual level—into the primary crisis of basic trust. In a real (though qualified) sense, religious experience, as Erikson points out, retraces man's earliest inner experiences, giving tangible form to vague evils and reaching back to the earliest moments of childhood. The child must learn to

[6] Johannes Lindworsky, S.J., *The Psychology of Asceticism* (Westminster: Newman, 1950), p. 15.

trust its parents. The religious man must learn to trust God. Only then can he venture out into the apparent void which lack of possessions means to his natural understanding and to his provident instincts. Otherwise he falls into a new and much worse predicament.

For man has a creative purpose. Even in the contemporary world, he is in some analogous way to fashion his life from nature, to control and dominate nature's forces and to draw from them his nourishment. The religious man relinquishes this struggle, and consequently relinquishes one of his most fundamental means of attaining complete manhood. He risks becoming irresponsible, childishly dependent on others who have been more successful in overcoming nature than he has been.

This is the basis of the crisis involved in the religious man's vow of poverty. Failure to resolve this crisis results in an infantile fear, a lack of responsibility. But when a man adopts poverty maturely, when he resolves the crisis attending such a vow, he learns to take daily action to keep alive his trust in God. And from the constantly reiterated confirmation of this trust he will draw nourishment for his love of God.

Voluntary poverty is an attempt to live so strongly upon the inner surge of love for Christ that external supports are reduced to a minimum. It is an attempt to be as much as possible. And from this base of being, the man of God works for good and attains the happiness of being what he is. Poverty gives man the power of spirit to operate without hindrance and ultimately to realize his unique self-identity.

But this demands the fullness of the vow. In our times and in our country, the spirit of the vow of poverty is in serious jeopardy. For it is extremely difficult to attain to the perfection of the vow of poverty (and therefore to resolve the crisis it poses to one's spiritual and psychological

maturity) under conditions of material prosperity. Very
few who take the vow of poverty in our country have to beg
for their next meal or sleep on park benches. As in a
former age, it is often the case that those who vow poverty
live in a state of comparative wealth possessing riches—in
the words of St. Bernard—"so great as even rich folk in the
world have not."

Yet the tradition of spiritual writing on religious poverty
states consistently that those who have only interior poverty run the risk of having none at all. The poor man always
feels caught in a network of constraints. If the religious
man calls himself poor and feels only the advantages of a
common life, if he finds all of his wishes completely satisfied, he can hardly be said to be living the vow of poverty
in its fullness.

The man who has the spirit of poverty will be extraor-
dinarily careful of material things, actually using incon-
venient and awkward things which cost him more time
and work than better ones. He will prefer cheap clothes
and shoes to more expensive ones, which would perhaps
last longer. The vow of poverty is not a vow of economy.
St. Francis wanted the houses of his Order to be made out
of wood, even in countries where stone buildings were less
expensive.[7] Thrift and economy suggest a natural wisdom
produced by worrying about this world's goods. Poverty is
a disposition of soul detaching man from these goods and
from anxiety concerning them: "for your Father knows
that you need all these things" (Matt. 6:32). This is not to
deny a place to natural prudence—merely to give it its
rightful place in the hierarchy of values.

Christian detachment demands, of course, a constant
struggle. The creatures of this world are not evil, but are

[7] Pius-Raymond Regamey, O.P., *Poverty* (New York: Sheed and
Ward, 1950), p. 162.

good in themselves. The man of God does not flee them or the worries and responsibilities they carry with them. Rather he seeks to restore the right kind of order to his own life and to his relations with God and other men. Ultimately Christian poverty has one purpose: to be more a man, as completely and as perfectly as possible. Failure to achieve such manhood, failure to realize one's own identity as a man, is the danger of the vow of poverty.

Chastity also entails a crisis. The religious community risks becoming an assembly of old bachelors or old maids, where egoism and selfishness are concealed behind a facade of virtue and piety. The crisis often has its genesis in false generosity or external pressures which prompt a young person to decide upon his vocation without any realization of the renunciation demanded by religious life. The individual has never faced the question of marriage or discerned the legitimate joys it offers. He only becomes aware of the beauty and joy of married life when it is too late to turn back.

For such a person the choice of the religious life becomes a regretted choice. There are serious vocational crises. Although these are perhaps never externalized, there is a deep sense of internal grievance, a feeling of confinement, of sorrow, and often of bitterness. Typically such a person comes to feel unconsciously that he is no longer bound to pursue the ideal he once set before himself. He turns within, and seeks to live as comfortable and humanly happy a life as may be salvaged from the environment in which he finds himself unwillingly imprisoned.

There is another danger inherent in the vow of chastity. This is the danger of a childish, emotional immaturity. It is the risk a man runs when he chooses to freely condemn his own manly life-giving powers to frustration and sterility. The crisis is only resolved by the cultivation of a sincere

desire for the virtue of chastity and by the development of
solid intellectual and volitional habits. Ultimately there
must be an integral chastity originating in a mature personality.

For religious chastity cannot arise from a condemnation
of one's natural powers. It must be grounded, not in the
rejection of a good mistakenly seen to be evil, but in the
choice of a greater good—in the choice of God. In the religious life it is God alone who is the bond; and the common life cannot be sanctified except insofar as the person,
by loving God, passes beyond its merely natural aspects.
The affection the religious man finds is therefore a fundamentally spiritual affection—one which leaves certain
sides of the human personality unsatisfied. There is friendship, even familial affection, in religious life. But the
mainstay of the family is conjugal love. Men do not go to
religious life to find what is proper to the family. Basically,
a religious man's life is in God, and in God one is alone.
Fundamental solitude—God is the portion of his inherit-
ance.

Psychologically, this involves a sublimation of the most
radical type, yet Freud himself admitted its possibility and
its actual fulfillment in St. Francis of Assisi and others. A
new and different identity must be forged. "In order to
arrive at being everything, desire to be nothing," wrote St.
John of the Cross. This crisis involves, ultimately, surrender
of self-identity, and union and absorption into the identity
of Christ.

The vow of obedience entails an equally radical crisis.
The religious man's identity threatens to be submerged. In
its most fundamental meaning identity is intrinsically
linked with the choice of one's own destiny. Meeting his
own spirit, man meets the power within him that can give
purpose to his life. His identity is contingent upon this

choice. He arrives at the fullness of his manhood in the moment in which he achieves his chosen purpose in life.

The Judeans who heard of the Lord's dealings with Zachary asked of John the Baptist: "What then will this child be?" (Luke 1:66). This is the question asked of every child that comes into the world. No one can answer it but the child himself. As he grows and develops, he gradually gives his answer in a whole series of choices. Existentialist literature especially makes this point: man fashions what he is to be in the exercise of his own freedom. He chooses his own identity.

Yet by his vow of obedience the religious man apparently declines this freedom. He turns aside from his encounter with himself, his identity, his spirit, and his powers of choice. Seemingly, he has rejected his right to fashion his own self-identity, to choose and determine for himself what he is to be. To many this is a scandal. It hits against a notion central in contemporary American Protestantism: the right and duty of man to determine his own conduct and to profit or suffer by the consequences. William James could not even imaginatively comprehend how free men, men possessing an inner life of their own, could come to think the subjection of their will to another finite creature recommendable.[8] To him this was something of a mystery, and to the majority of contemporary thinkers it is equally unintelligible.

But the crisis for the religious man is not one of submitting his will to that of other finite creatures. The religious man empties himself of his will in an act which consecrates it to God. Finite creatures embody, through the authority given them in Christ's Church, the will of God. The real crisis of religious obedience is that involved in

[8] William James, *The Varieties of Religious Experience* (New York: Longmans, Green, 1909), p. 311.

freely surrendering the right to be self-directed in one's
own choices. The religious man risks purposelessness. He
must be constantly on his guard not to yield to the comfortable feeling that all responsibility is the superior's.
There is the permanent temptation to flee the agonies of
decision, to act only when and as commanded. There need
be no searching of conscience to discover powers and abilities not exploited. The individual need have no aspirations.
In short, there is the danger of inertia.

The only possible resolution of this crisis is that gained
through absolute and total obedience. There is a paradox
here. The religious man empties himself of his own will,
and at that moment the whole world enters in to fill the
vacant space. In this sense it is true that the man of God
has no particular desires. His one desire is to be allowed
to disappear—to reveal to mankind in his own person, as
light through an invisible pane of glass, the world as God
has willed it. Yet more than any other man the religious
man is responsible. He is aware of his obligation to choose
for himself. He cannot merely do what another person says
he must do. He must do what he sees to be God's will. The
responsibility is his own—the terrible responsibility of
choosing consistently the choice of God.

Ultimately it is a question of love. Everything must be
done from love; nothing, from routine. Above all, nothing
must be done from fear. This was one of the insights of St.
Francis de Sales. "You must love obedience more than you
fear disobedience," he wrote to Madame de Chantal. For
religious obedience has no meaning unless it originates in
a conscious and reflective love.

There is one other aspect of the identity crisis in religious
life, the professional aspect. There are two sides of the identity crisis: achievement of personal identity and achieve-

ment of social identity. What precisely constitutes the religious man's growth in personal identity has been discussed in some detail. There is also the social rôle of many religious men and women in American society today, their rôle of teacher and scholar.

Much has been written and much said about the plight of the American Catholic educational endeavor. One facet of these discussions is of interest here: the undeniable need of Catholic educators to dedicate themselves completely to the subjects they teach. This dedication must mean a commitment of the sort which involves the individual completely in the field he is interested in, so much so that he is eager and enthusiastic to see and to contribute to its progress. And since there is no way to dedicate oneself to learning from the outside, the individual must devote himself totally to his field. A bystander is too uncommitted.

Yet if there is anything that American Catholic education suffers from it is that too few religious men and women are totally committed to the subjects they profess.[9] Instead of seeing total dedication to professional competence as part of religious dedication to God, they allow a needless conflict to develop which hinders both professional and religious excellence.

A certain amount of rôle conflict is inevitable for the religious man who is also a professional scholar and educator. The religious organization is necessarily bureaucratic in its functionings. The bureaucracy imposes upon the individual a rôle and corresponding norms. The professional educator also has his rôle with its norms. These two sets of rôles and norms are at times in diametrical opposition to each other.

[9] Walter J. Ong, S.J., *American Catholic Crossroads* (New York: Macmillan, 1959), pp. 104–105.

The bureaucratic mode of organization requires:

    (1) centralized leadership
    (2) emphasis on procedure
    (3) simplification of tasks
    (4) little initiative
    (5) corporate responsibility
    (6) impersonal relations
    (7) ascribed status
    (8) service to the system.

The professional mode of organization requires:

    (1) leadership of expertness
    (2) variability of procedures
    (3) totality of tasks
    (4) broad initiative
    (5) personal responsibility
    (6) close colleague relations
    (7) achieved status
    (8) service to the client.[10]

The conflict is heightened by the individual's realization that in attaining professional competence he cuts himself off to a certain extent from the religious organization, achieving prestige in an outside group that knows nothing of his other rôle. At the same time his professional achievements often cannot be accurately evaluated by superiors and other members of his religious community.

The individual may attempt to resolve such rôle conflicts by unrealistically endeavoring to lead two lives—one inside and the other outside of the religious community. More frequently, there is a slow drift in one direction or the other, until the individual finds that he must surrender the attempt to achieve professional excellence or modify his religious ideals, becoming satisfied with half-hearted and

[10] Joseph H. Fichter, S.J., *Religion as an Occupation* (Notre Dame, Ind.: Notre Dame Univer. Press, 1961), pp. 224–225.

mediocre accomplishment of the duties and obligations of his religious state.

Such rôle conflicts, of course, seriously jeopardize the resolution of the individual's identity crisis. It would seem that many religious men and women, who have to a great extent resolved admirably the problems of personal vocational identity, have not resolved the problems of social identity, have not seen clearly their own rôle as teachers and scholars. Perhaps the opposite is often true, but in either case it is apparent that there is need for a successful resolution of the identity crisis on both levels and for an integration at an even higher level.

This integration can be achieved only when the religious man realizes that it is false and misleading to distinguish between competence in his religious rôle and competence in his professional rôle, between growth in personal holiness and growth in the knowledge of chemistry, mathematics, or physics. There will necessarily be conflicts—often irresolvable and frustrating conflicts. This will introduce a certain amount of psychological tension into the individual's practical life. But the attainment of one's spiritual ideals is not something apart from attainment of professional competence. The religious man whose work is performed in obedience to Christ, in union with Christ, and for the purpose of Christ, finds in his service the source of his sanctity. His own judgment, the intimations given him by the Holy Spirit, and the commands of obedience—these determine the nature and extent of his service and, consequently, of his holiness. It is precisely in this form of service that he is to find his sanctity. Even the psychological tension rôle conflicts create can be used to augment this sanctity.

The greatness of man consists in his origin, his nobility

as a creature, as a child of God. But more than this: there is also his unique vocation. Man is called upon to cooperate with the divine liberty in the creation of his own identity. This involves a process of what Dietrich von Hildebrand calls "confronting all things with Christ."[11] The saint alone has solved the identity crisis perfectly. He has transformed his self-identity into the identity of Christ. Each saint is a prism of glass of a different structure through which Christ's radiance shines. But all men are called to be saints. And since psychological maturity is normally prerequisite to sanctity, the resolution of the identity crisis prepares the way for religious growth.

It is often said that the child stabilizes the family. After the first few years of marriage the love of the honeymoon is ordinarily exhausted. A new love unfolds. Ideally, it is the affection both parents share for the child that forms the basis of this new—and more mature—bond of conjugal love.

Perhaps a similar phenomenon occurs in religious life. After the first four or five years (or even much later since circumstances and persons differ) a process of reintegration takes place. The religious person must re-examine and re-interpret his initial motives and goals. A newer, fresher love must supplant the older, faded love. And because the natural aids which married life affords are lacking, this transformation to a higher and more perfect love requires supernatural grace and natural maturity.

During this period the religious man must struggle with forces obstructing and counteracting the resolution of his personal vocational identity. The crisis is resolved gradually as the individual resolves the separate crises associated with each of the vows. Ultimately, as in marriage, there is a

[11] Dietrich von Hildebrand, *Transformation in Christ* (New York: Longmans, Green, 1948), p. 74.

transformation of love, and a newer, more mature love becomes established.

There is a continuity in life which the saint makes manifest. The child persists in the man. The mature adult has grown out of childhood without losing childhood's best traits. He retains the basic emotional strengths and the stubborn autonomy of the infant, the capacity for wonder and pleasure and playfulness of the preschool years, the capacity for affiliation and the intellectual curiosity of the school years, and the idealism and passion of adolescence. He has incorporated these into a new pattern dominated by adult stability, wisdom, responsibility, and prudence.

The saint does not live apart from the happenings of everyday life. He is not a man in communion with God and out of communion with other men. Because he lives in close contact with God, because he has conformed his mind to the mind of Christ, the saint is the one man who is in communion with us, while all others live apart.

This is why the saint is the perfectly mature individual, at once the most sensitive and the most spiritual of men. He is the most sensitive because nothing and no one in the world finds him irresponsive, since he is always in immediate and loving contact with persons and things. He is the most spiritual of men, for every movement of his personality has its origin in the realization that Christ is the measure of all things, the source of his own identity.

Intimacy

4 There is an old saying that life begins when childhood and adolescence come to an end. The individual is by this time prepared to enter upon his career, to settle down in marriage, and to raise a family of his own. Relations with members of the opposite sex take on a new tone as the person seriously prepares to choose a partner to share his life. A new sense of intimacy develops as two young people grow in love. They learn to accept each other as persons and to yield selfish and egocentric desires when these conflict with those of the future husband or wife. In the intimacy of their relationship the individuals experience a gradual deepening and opening of personality.

Such intimacy is possible only after a reasonable sense of personal identity has been established. The young person who has no sure sense of identity shies away from close interpersonal relations. The surer he becomes of himself, however, the more he seeks them. As his identity becomes delineated, the person can go out to others and interact with them on a level far more human and meaningful than was possible before. Traces of self-centered thought are gradually eradicated as the individual learns to deal with others respectfully and, ultimately, lovingly.

Paradoxically, identity often develops simultaneously with a growing capacity for personal intimacy. The adolescent attachment between a boy and girl is often no more

64

than an attempt to establish a definition of personal identity by endless conversation, mutual confession of feelings
and conflicts, and discussion of wishes, plans, and expectations. When a young person does not in some way engage in
such intimate relations with others—especially of the type
which tends to promote such identity formation—there
may be flight or repeated frustration. The individual may
seek to isolate himself from others, developing highly
stereotyped and formal interpersonal relations. Or there
may be the experience of repeated attempts to attain intimate interpersonal relations and repeated failures. In
either case, the outcome is the same. The individual's relationship with others lacks all spontaneity and warmth. He
becomes incapable of a real and mutual exchange of love.

Erikson calls such an outcome "distantiation,"[1] or isolation and self-absorption. There is a readiness to repudiate,
to isolate, and even to destroy those forces and people
whose presence seems to threaten one's security. Other
people seem to impinge upon the individual, to challenge
his freedom, to make incessant demands upon him.

Perhaps such an attitude has its roots, not merely in an
uncertainty concerning personal identity, but in early
childhood experiences as well. The continuity of life is
reflected in the individual whose childhood egocentrism
has never been subdued. Social conventions may render
such self-centered behavior dormant in certain circumstances, but it appears unmistakably whenever the individual is called on to freely assist others or when he is faced
with the opportunity to perform a thoughtful and selfless
action. For many people earlier selfish automatisms have
never been replaced by mature habits of charity toward
others.

[1] Erik H. Erikson, *Identity and the Life Cycle* (New York: International Univ. Press, 1959), p. 95.

But the problem is not merely a personal one. It is above all a social problem, one characteristic of modern life generally. Within the framework of modern culture, man is constantly dealing with man in a manner that is basically inhuman. The complexity of modern life aggravates depersonalization, forcing the individual to become a slave of a mechanical master. People may live for years without knowing who their next-door neighbors are. Men work next to other men and never see their neighbor as a person, but merely as another part of the shop or factory. Modern life is a life from which personal relationships and a natural living interest in people have been methodically excluded, and to this extent it is an unreal and unhealthy life.

Consequently, the conditions of modern living seriously jeopardize the resolution of the crisis of intimacy. Often young people who have not resolved the crisis of intimacy will enter marriage, hoping to find in this state an escape from the depersonalizing influences of contemporary society or from their own psychological inadequacies. They hope to find themselves in finding their partner. But the tower has been built without a foundation, and it is likely to crumble. If the individual has not developed his capacity for intimate interpersonal relations before marriage, it is in most cases too late to begin. Habits of selfishness have dropped their roots too deeply into the layers of personality. There is a sacramental character to marriage, but here again grace cooperates with nature.

If a sense of intimacy is attained with difficulty in married life, it is perhaps even more problematic for the individual in religious life. In religious life—presupposing normal adolescent development prior to entrance—the individual resolves the crisis of intimacy in his dealings with his fellow religious. It is through the friendships which grow out of these dealings with one another that the religious man develops his sense of intimacy. Yet these friendships are of a special type—based ultimately upon spiritual values. There is necessarily an admixture of the natural, but the supernatural must always have pre-eminence. Consequently, intimate interpersonal relations in religious life presuppose a certain spiritual maturity, and this in turn demands optimal emotional maturity.

Emotional maturity is a somewhat ambiguous concept. It is relative to the stage of development in which the individual finds himself, but in general denotes the attainment of a certain healthy balance between extreme emotional states. It suggests the possession of definite qualities which enable the person to preserve peace within himself and with others. These qualities include such characteristics as decisive thinking, unselfishness, a sense of personal responsibility for the common good, temperate emotional reactions, a well-balanced attitude regarding sex, ability to profit from criticism, and the ability to face reality.[2]

Although any attempt to spell out the characteristics of emotional maturity is to a certain extent arbitrary, the possession of the qualities mentioned is indicative of the capacity to enter upon friendships which will deepen one's personal sense of intimacy and which will serve to increase self-knowledge. And since this sense of intimacy results from healthy and mature friendship, it would seem imperative for the religious man to foster and enjoy such friendships if he is to grow in psychological and ultimately spiritual maturity.

Not all friendship, of course, develops a sense of intimacy. Often what is called friendship is actually fellowship—that type of interaction which rests on reciprocal interests or

[2] Gerald Kelly, S.J., *Guidance for Religious* (Westminster: Newman, 1956), pp. 6 ff.

mutual advantage. Here the primary motive is selfish, although not necessarily consciously so. Or there is a type of interpersonal relationship which has a primarily lubricative function—it keeps the organization or the community going without unnecessary and unfortunate friction.

But friendship which terminates in a mature sense of intimacy is characterized by fidelity, a certain trust, and mutual acceptance. There is a consistent forbearance, an ability on the part of the two persons to overlook transitory moods and passing emotional states. There is trust, since both parties are willing to allow the other person to see weaknesses and failings, hopes and aspirations. And there is a certain sense of equality which prevents a one-way admiration from developing. For if one individual serves as the model, guide, and ideal for the other, it becomes more a discipleship than a friendship. In spite of respective gifts of nature or grace, true friendship is always marked by mutual acceptance.

If friendship is of this nature, it can play two major rôles in the development of the religious man: it can strengthen his chastity and deepen his love.

In Freudian theory the term "sublimation" refers to the gratification of unattained sexual desires through substitutive nonsexual activities, or to the gratification of unattained aggressive desires through substitutive nonaggressive activities. Theoretically, sublimation is based upon the utilization of general physiological energy in constructive behavior which indirectly reduces the tension built up around frustrated sexual or aggressive drives. So conceived, sublimation has considerable cultural value in producing socially approved activity when strong drives are frustrated.

Whatever the true nature of the mechanisms involved, some such sublimation must be achieved in religious life.

Even on a natural level, Freud believed that the most perfect form of happiness available to man was that attained by those men who had managed to sublimate merely sexual love and transform it into a love which embraced all men equally. Such individuals, he thought, have arrived at the highest state of mind man is capable of achieving.

For love cannot terminate in one person. If it does, it most probably is not love at all, but an expanded egoism. Most people, however, are of the opinion that love is constituted by the object, not by the faculty. Love is considered to be most intense when it is fixated on the one loved person. Frequently those who have never loved anyone are inwardly convinced that they will immediately learn to love as soon as the right person comes along. Such an attitude is comparable to that of a man who wants to paint and who is convinced that he will learn as soon as he finds the right object. Then he will paint, and paint beautifully. Unfortunately, painting is an art and must be developed. To paint well, the individual must be able to paint many objects. In the same way, to be capable of truly loving another person, the individual must develop his love; he must be capable of loving all men. If he is to sincerely love one person, he must learn to love the world.[3]

The religious man deliberately chooses to be nailed to the cross of the world. The sublimation this requires is ultimately attained when his love for God is transformed and extended to a love which embraces all men. Christ is his model, and it is in His chastity that the religious man finds the ideal of his own.

Natural, human friendship plays an important part in the acquisition of this sublimated love of God and man. Perhaps there are times in the life of an individual when it is only in man and through personal exchange with man

[3] Fromm, *op. cit.*, p. 46.

that he glimpses a reality beyond man. Certainly it is
through friendship and the consequent sense of intimacy
which friendship brings that the personality is expanded
and arrives ultimately at its fullest growth.

But unless the necessary sublimation has been effected
and natural love is transformed into a supernatural charity,
friendship involves a certain risk. This, in the context of
the religious life, constitutes the essence of the crisis of
intimacy. It is difficult to love others out of supernatural
charity. It is easy to love them for many other reasons,
natural and noble enough, but which inspire a love that is-
sues from natural motives more than from love of God and
authentic charity.

The friendship that exists between religious men must,
therefore, be a sublimated and supernaturalized friendship.
In a certain sense, love always has God as its object. But it
is not enough merely to pay lip service to this truth. There
must be the corresponding effort to see Christ in the other
person, or at least to see the other person as Christ would
see him. Admittedly, all friendship contains a sensible aspect. It is typically founded upon a similarity of temperament and mutual interests. It is spiritually pure only when
one's love for Christ is pure. As the individual becomes
more and more capable of such pure love of Christ, he
becomes capable of more perfect friendship and of the
healthy sense of intimacy that such friendship engenders.
If this sublimation is not achieved, the intimacy crisis is
left unresolved, to the detriment of the individual's psychological and spiritual development.

Traditionally, ascetical writers have set down norms concerning friendship. These relate particularly to the danger
that such intimacy creates for the religious man who has
dedicated his love totally to Christ in the vow of chastity.
The warning against harmful friendships is necessary, al-

though perhaps exaggerated. Generally such signs of false and imperfect friendship are listed as exclusiveness, continual thought of the friend, jealousy, restlessness of mind in the friend's absence, blindness to apparent faults in the friend, and so forth.

Another danger, although one which pertains more to community charity than to the individual's vow of chastity, is the danger of small cliques. This constitutes a counterfeit of authentic friendship and one that is incompatible with religious life. While it is true that the individual will inevitably feel closer to some people and will be able to speak more freely and confidently with these than with others, it is also true that the man of God excludes no one from his charity.

Universal charity is one of the central messages of the Gospel. If love for others has achieved its supernatural quality, it will be marked by universality. This is the necessary consequence of a love based on the divine Paternity and man's supernatural brotherhood. Without this, love is basically false and perhaps harmful.

However, to insist upon the dangers of unhealthy or exclusive forms of friendship can be misleading, and can even have very serious ill effects. Often awareness of the dangers involved will tend to generate a fear of any friendship. The religious man may come to condemn friendship in his own life and to suspect it in the lives of others. There is considerable danger attached to the avoidance and suspicion of friends. Admittedly, complete rejection of friendship enables the individual to avoid the risks associated with it, but typically such strategy leads to greater dangers.

There have been saints who have attained great holiness through the sacrifice of human affection. For these men and women any friendship involved a preference for the creature over the Creator. As such it was seen to be an imperfection, incompatible with total love of God. Heroically, such individuals closed their hearts to human friends so that they might open them more completely to God.

But these are the exceptions, and it may be strongly suspected that, in the final stages of their spiritual development, such individuals found in God a greater freedom to love fellow men. More typically, the attempt to carry this cross has ended in spiritual disaster. Where a few have succeeded, the vast majority suffer deep and lasting injury from seeking to reach God along the path of loneliness. They find that in the end they are incapable of loving God or man. Or they suffer the revenge of a thwarted and repressed human nature which suddenly revolts, presenting the individual with almost irresistible temptations which may require a lifetime to conquer or may themselves conquer the individual. Where these extreme outcomes are avoided, the person often finds himself devoid of joy, unable to express warmth, even incapable of smiling.[4] This is the danger of which St. Francis de Sales spoke. "One must not push this caution to excess," he wrote of the fear of friendship, "because by force of the wish to stifle all natural love, one may end by extinguishing charity itself. If one blows too violently, the nose bleeds."

An exclusive friendship does threaten the chastity of the religious man—at least the perfection of the virtue. He has sacrificed the normal emotional outlets which other young people find in married life. Sublimation is not easily attained, and the individual feels the natural tendency to seek emotional relief and compensation in exclusive friendship. Nevertheless, if it is not exclusive and if it is not marked by any of the other characteristics of unhealthy

[4] René Voillaume, *Seeds of the Desert* (Chicago: Fides, 1955), pp. 313–314.

attachment, the religious man will not be hindered, but rather helped through friendship.

Normally, man cannot live a fully mature life without friendship. He finds himself from the very beginning in social interaction with other persons. When he attains physical independence of other people, he still has a psychological need for their support. And if he is to escape selfishness and isolation, he has a psychological need for intimacy with others. "Nothing can be compared to a faithful friend: and no weight of gold and silver is able to countervail the goodness of his fidelity" (Sirach 6:15). The human support the religious man finds in intimate friendship is one of the greatest of life's blessings. St. Gregory Nazianzen once wrote that if he were asked what is the most beautiful thing in life, he would answer that it is to have a friend.

Essentially unnatural or supernatural, religious life is in a certain sense a life of violence. The sublimation and transformation it entails is radical and naturally difficult for man. The danger of emotional immaturity plagues the religious man who has consecrated himself to one Love by his vow of chastity. Gradually through constant self-control, the cultivation of an abiding sense of the presence of God, and an increasingly generous love, the religious person must learn to live entirely for God. This is the perfection of his chastity.

And religious friendship can be of great assistance in this process. When the religious man has the comfort and support of friendship, he normally tends to regret less what he has surrendered. The process of sublimation is facilitated, and there is a greater contentment and natural joy in religious life. Without the consolation of friendship the religious man is likely to experience, perhaps unconsciously, severe emotional starvation. Such a condition results in tension and ultimately seriously threatens the perfection of the individual's chastity. There is ordinarily no grave danger, but there is a chiseling off; the individual goes about anxiously seeking sources of emotional compensation.[5] This leads inevitably to spiritual mediocrity and a gravitation toward the natural.

While loneliness may mark the life of the religious man, it is not his fundamental option. He chooses God and God alone. But this does not mean that the individual vows to live his life without other people. There is an essential loneliness, but one which permits the closest of friendships. There is a greater risk to chastity in the sacrifice of such friendship than there is in its cultivation. Through trust in others and intimate dealings with them the man of God will ordinarily gain strength and confidence to live his life of the vows. Normally, friendship provides the religious man with a source of inspiration, a means to grow in grace and virtue. The exchange that friendship demands is for the religious man an exchange which helps him to grow in his love for Christ. It generates mutual encouragement and consolation, even a spiritual competitiveness which drives both persons on to higher perfection—to a more trusting poverty, a more integral chastity, a more responsible and loving obedience.

Yet there will be moments of keen loneliness. This is true in the lives of married people as well. However, the religious man has an advantage. For even if there are periods when human friendship is lacking, he is never entirely alone.

Consequently, there must be a thoughtful tension between loneliness in God and intimacy with others. If his

[5] Columban Browning, C.P., "Friendship among Religious," *Review for Religious*, 18 (1959), 261.

charity is universal in its scope and if the negative norms
for friendship are applied, the religious man will find his
friends decidedly helpful. They will assist him in his chastity, particularly by providing him with a natural outlet for
healthy and necessary emotional satisfaction and by lend-
ing him support and encouragement. Perhaps the discouragement and tension which result from failure to ob-
tain legitimate emotional release create the greatest blocks
to the psychological and spiritual progress of the religious
man. The isolation which such failure produces tends to
turn the individual in upon himself, posing a threat to his
chastity and restricting his capacity to love his fellow men.
It is precisely here that friendship is the most help. Yet it
is also true that a certain sense of isolation, of basic loneliness, is spiritually beneficial. This serves as a constant re-
minder to the religious man that God is a jealous God, and
that his love for other men must be grounded first of all in
love of God.

The second major function friendship plays in the development of the religious man is to deepen his charity.
Mention was made previously of a paradox characteristic of
much of modern art and literature. While modern life in-
tensifies and augments a deleterious process of depersonalization and dehumanization, no other age has been so self-
conscious and so aware of the uniqueness and importance of
the individual person.

This emphasis on the person is, of course, central in the
Christian notion of charity. In fact, this was what gave
Christian love its revolutionary tone. The Greeks had a
notion of social affection between members of the city-state
and later a notion of ecstatic love in the mystery cults. But
the concept of personal love was generally absent from
their thought. Even the love which characterized Judaism

was somewhat impersonal—expressed in social conventions
or in individual prayer to an awesome and fearful God.
There was little of the peace and joy which characterize
the exchange between persons. But Christian love focuses
upon the individual. It is a love of exchange, selfless and
devoted to the service of God and one's neighbor. Modern
interest and emphasis on the person merely reflect this dis-
tinctly Christian concern for persons.

Christ addressed Himself to individual persons, not to
mankind in general: "Come to me, all you who labor and
are burdened, and I will give you rest" (Matt. 11:28).
Consequently, the religion of the Christian is based on
personal needs and is directed toward the fulfillment of
these needs by a Person. And the charity of the Christian is
characterized by emphasis upon the personal worth of each
individual man. The Christian loves all men because they
are all sons of a common Father.

This is the original challenge of Christian charity. It is
easy to love mankind as an abstraction, but it is almost impossible to love one's neighbor as a concrete individual.
This is why Chesterton felt that Christian charity involved
the essentially unreasonable requirement of pardoning un-
pardonable acts and loving unlovable people.

An authentic Christian love for other persons is not primarily concerned with their qualities. The individual is not
loved because of the traits of character that he possesses.
His selfhood is not merely grasped in a variety of impersonal qualities and attributes that might equally well be
found in others. Rather what is loved is the center of the
person's being, the uniqueness of his identity, the root of
his personality. It is spirit, and the spiritual is always in-
communicable. This is the reason why the expressions of
two young people in love are unending. It is because their
object is ineffable.

The German poet, Rainer Maria Rilke, spoke occasionally of the dull, blank emptiness which stares out of animals' eyes. The animal is a living creature without self-consciousness, without personality. He symbolizes for the poet the condition of modern man in his vain attempt to penetrate to the self-consciousness of others. There is the knowledge, at least indirect knowledge, that such self-consciousness exists; but modern man feels himself to be totally isolated in a world of real personalities, incapabale of communicating his self-consciousness or of intimately registering that of others.[6] Language, William Faulkner once wrote, is a meager and fragile thread by which the little surface corners and edges of men's secret and solitary lives are joined for an instant, only to sink back into the inevitable darkness. Occasionally a man will catch a glimpse of the spiritual center of another's personality as it momentarily rises to the surface. But such moments are rare. Consequently, the brute animal, totally devoid of self-consciousness, impressively symbolizes modern man's isolation.

The difficulties man faces in attaining intimate relation and communication with other men constitute a problem basic to Christian charity. It is a problem of importance to the Christian because it is only when man becomes conscious of himself, of his own uniqueness as a creature and, through grace, a son of God, that he is capable of redemption. Only when he grasps his own identity in this way does man come to realize that he is different from the plant and the animal. At this moment he grasps his spiritual nature.

But this grasp of the spiritual is only secured through communication of knowledge and love with God and man. Communication is the path to the truth of one's own

[6] Walter J. Ong, S.J., "St. Ignatius' Prison-cage and the Existentialist Situation," *Theological Studies*, 25 (1954), p. 44.

uniqueness. Man only grasps fully his essential nature, his own proper selfhood, when he is in the presence of, and cherishes, the identity and selfhood of another. This is why the resolution of the crisis of identity is bound up with the resolution of the crisis of intimacy.

Yet modern man finds that intimate communication is rarely possible. Even those who are closest to him physically seem infinitely remote. Man's words miss the mark. They hit the target inches too low or fall far short. For this reason personality in man seems to be linked with affliction, and the attempt to communicate with love seems impossible.

But life without intimate communication, without friendship, is basically inhuman and a danger to personal development. In spite of the difficulties of communication, man must become conscious of himself in his uniqueness and of others in their uniqueness. Otherwise, there is no grasp of one's own identity and no respect for the selfhood of others. Charity is impossible, and therefore Christian life is impossible. There is only a selfish and isolated individualism.

The antonym of Christian charity is individualism. Properly speaking, this refers to a system of morals, feelings, ideas, and institutions in which individuals are organized according to principles intended to guarantee mutual isolation and unlimited freedom. The first condition of such a system is the centralization of the individual in himself. This is in radical contrast to Christian charity and to the doctrine of personalism characteristic of much of modern thought.

Personalism insists upon the decentralization of the personality. The person exists only toward others, and finds his own identity only in knowing others and in being

known by them. All real living, Martin Buber would say, is
meeting. The *thou* (to employ the terminology of personalism) is prior to the *I* and implies a *we*. It is precisely
here, in this union of two spirits, that the individual discovers his own spiritual resources. When such communication fails or is corrupted, the individual suffers an essential
loss. He becomes a stranger to himself, alienated. In this
sense, the crisis of intimacy is almost metaphysical. Man
exists only insofar as he exists for others. To be, in the
final analysis, is to love.[7]

Personalism has attempted to delineate carefully the slow
transition which occurs as love develops between two persons who then begin to exist to each other and to themselves.
The *thou* becomes *thou* more and more profoundly. Initially, however, one encounters a *him*. A man may, for example, meet a stranger on the train. They speak of the
weather, of international politics, and so forth. The relationship may terminate here. The two leave each other as
strangers. Or they may meet again and gradually come to
know more and more of each other's biography. Slowly
there is communication. They learn of each other's interests,
aspirations, ideals. Each individual becomes aware of the
self-consciousness of the other, of his absolute "unrelated-
ness." This leads to self-knowledge and ultimately to genuine love.

Human life and personal identity come into existence in
such intimate communication. Here the person learns not
merely who he is, but that he is limited, cast upon his own
finitude. He needs others to complement him, yet he possesses his own unique relation to truth. The person makes
his appearance in relation to other persons. Men need, and
attain through friendship, confirmation in their individ-

[7] Emmanuel Mounier, *Personalism* (New York: Grove Press, 1952),
p. 20.

uality, in their own truth as this reflects the Divine inten-
tion in their regard. This at least is the contention of
personalism.

Yet the influence of the contemporary individualistic society works so strongly upon modern man that he becomes
unable to interact with others in a basically human way.
Consequently, he is afraid of not being loved; but the real,
though unconscious, fear is that of loving. He has learned
to fear to love and has become locked up in his egoism. Yet
he seeks some means of escape: "I'm sick of ego, ego, ego.
My own and everybody's." Salinger's Franny Glass merely
echoes the sentiments of millions of men and women in our
society. And the only escape from individualism is a personalism grounded upon a sincere Christian concern for persons.

This is why friendship is so important in religious life.
The old scholastic maxim still has force: no one gives what
he does not have. If he is to offer modern man a meaningful answer to life, one that will enable him to attain selfhood, identity, the fullness of love, the religious man must
himself have experienced what Gabriel Marcel calls the
condition of community, whereby two people become *thou*
for each other. Founded in Christ's love and elevated by
grace, the perfection of charity is the Christian solution to
the dilemma which contemporary life sets before man.
Without this solution modern man has only the choice of
becoming engulfed in ego, surrendering the possibility
of love, or of sinking to the level of *it*, losing possession of
personal identity.

The perfection of Christian charity, which is before all
else the mark of the Christian and the duty of the religious
man, requires the cultivation of several fundamental attitudes. These are ordinarily acquired in the intimate rela-

tionship that exists between friends. Once they have been
assimilated into his personal value system, the religious
man is capable of preaching the message that he of all men
must preach to the modern world.

The first of these is the attitude of presence. To be incapable of presence is to be in some way preoccupied with
one's own self. The immediate object of such concern may
be any one of a number of things: health, possessions, talents, even spiritual perfection. It is not so much the object
which is of importance, but the manner in which the person is concerned about the object. There is a withdrawal, an
excessive attachment, which cuts the individual off from
other persons.

Opposed to this is a state of detachment. It is not a state
of emptiness or bored indifference, but a state in which the
individual knows that he is not his own and assumes an authentic, Christian orientation toward others. He is at the
disposal of others, consecrated to them and interrelated to
all men alike. In some intangible way he presents himself
to others. He is not merely an attentive and conscientious
listener. He does not merely sympathize. For there is a way
of listening and a way of sympathizing that is basically a
refusal of oneself, and there is another way of listening
and a way of sympathizing that is a way of giving. The
attitude of presence is something which reveals itself immediately and unmistakably in a look, a smile, an intona-
tion, or a handshake.[8]

Closely related to the attitude of presence is the attitude
of availability. The individual is available to the extent that
he is detached from himself, decentralized, capable of going
out to others, and receptive and open to them. He is free
for other persons. This involves the asceticism of self-

[8] Gabriel Marcel, *The Philosophy of Existence* (New York: Philosophical Library, 1949), pp. 26–28.

dispossession, an asceticism central to Christian life. In a
world of egocentricism, individualism, narcissism, the Christian bears witness to the selfless and open love of the Son
of God. The salvation which Christ offered mankind is repeatedly offered in the Christian's spontaneous love.

Antithetical to such an attitude is the attitude of pride.
Traditionally, pride is defined as an exaggeratedly good
opinion of oneself which arises from self-love. More fundamentally, pride consists in an unrealistic assertion of independence. The individual asserts that he is capable of
deriving all of his strength from himself. He thereby cuts
himself off from communion with other men, closing himself to them.

The humility of availability consists precisely in a sense
of freedom. The available man is free from egocentric self-
love and free to give himself to another person. He recognizes that to treat another person instrumentally, as a
source of information or as a means of obtaining emotional
gratification, is to behave toward him as though he were an
object, an *it*. In effect, this means despairing of him. But
to be present toward him and available to his needs is to
give him hope.

Another attitude essential to the perfection of Christian
charity is that of empathy. Other human beings, as persons,
cannot be treated as objects. As at least potentially sons of
God by grace, they must be loved in their being. This means
that the other person must be taken on—his troubles, joys,
and destiny must be shared. To participate in the being of
another person, as deeply and as meaningfully as is
humanly possible, it is necessary to relive his free acts, to
identify with his will, his love, and his whole being. This is
the essential note of a Christian empathy which, unlike a
condescending sympathy, consists primarily in identification.

This requires generosity, the attitude of giving. The generosity of self-bestowal has no limits and seeks no reward. It looks outward and seeks the good of the other. It is apparently irrational, characterized by forgiveness and kindness. Consequently, the attitude of generosity serves as the ultimate criterion of the authenticity of a person's love. Mere sentimentalism is not generous.

Finally, there is the attitude of fidelity. The adventure of charity continues until death. In this sense it parallels the continuity of the individual's own personality. It undergoes the same renewal processes, developing in time. It is contingent upon spatial and temporal conditions, yet it is enduring. In fact, the continuity of the individual's personality is dependent upon the continuity of his love. His identity, in its most meaningful expression, is found in relation to other persons. This is merely the undeniable consequence of man's natural and supernatural solidarity.

Such attitudes—presence, availability, empathy, generosity, fidelity—are the fundamental attitudes of Christian charity. Concretely, they are the attitudes of friendship, the characteristics of a friend. They are the marks of the charity of the religious man whose task it is to bear witness to the modern world of the possibility of love. To do this, he must experience friendship—a friendship grounded ultimately in his love of God. Here he will learn the attitudes basic to Christian love. Subsequently, he must seek to give his love for every man he meets the character and depth of his love of a friend.

In all of life's happenings, love is outstandingly unique. The ordinary events of everyday life introduce no disturbing elements into the depths of one's being, but the encounter with another seizes man at the very core of his personality. Such an experience is a necessity for his full development, but it may be wasted. The crisis of intimacy may be resolved by turning away—if so, the consequence is isolation. Or it may be resolved by turning toward—in which case the outcome is growth.

When two persons communicate with each other, each one experiences himself, grasps his own identity, and in the same instant becomes aware of the need to surrender this identity to the newly recognized identity of the other person. This is the basic fact of love. Experienced in this way, it presents a constant challenge. It is not a static state of peace, but a dynamic and growing interaction. There may be harmony or conflict, joy or sadness, pleasure or suffering. But essentially there must be union. The two individuals come to experience their oneness, to stand as *thou* to each other. Their love is secure because of the depth of the relationship which has been established. It is proven in the gradual selfless surrender of the two persons to each other.

Because of the self-surrender that it requires, love is a preparation for the surrender to God that religion requires. In this sense every love, as Max Scheler wrote, is love for God taking a rest by the wayside. In that process by which man is made aware of another, he becomes dimly aware of the eternal Person. In each *thou* he addresses, ultimately, the eternal *Thou*.

This accounts for the limitation of human love. Only in the Absolute is man able to love with full sufficiency. His temporal condition imposes a limitation because of the finitude of satisfaction offered by other creatures. But man may transcend this condition, and does in addressing the Person of the infinite God. Man's love for God—whether it be incipient and unrecognized or actual—is the source of all love and the ultimate source of its complete satisfaction.

This is why, of all men, the religious man is most capable of loving. Ideally, the charity of the religious man is consciously rooted in his love of God. It is therefore an authentic charity, the love of the Gospel, Christian in the fullest sense. But if the religious man is to bring this love to the modern world, if he is to fulfill his Christian mission, he must have experienced what it means to love. This is the rôle that friendship plays in the life of the religious man. This is why the intimacy crisis is of central importance to his development. For it is in his intimate dealings with his fellow men that he encounters the spiritual, and hopefully raises the other person to a spiritual plane. At each such personal encounter, originating in supernatural charity, the Gospel succeeds and Christianity is effective.

For the religious man, therefore, the crisis of intimacy is closely related to the life of the vows. It presents itself as problematic to his vow of chastity. He senses the need for intimate communication with other men, but realizes that he has consecrated his love to God. Somehow he must sublimate and transcend mere human affection for others and ground his love for them in his love for God. If this is achieved, he finds that friendship safeguards his chastity and provides him with a source of inspiration for spiritual progress.

But the crisis of intimacy is also problematic to his vow of poverty. For poverty, in its fullest meaning, is directed toward assuring openness, total disposability. It renders the individual accessible to the claims of men. Selfish isolation is the psychological counterpart of selfish attachment to material goods. It obstructs openness and stands in the way of the availability and generosity characteristic of the perfection of Christian charity.

Generativity

5 The crisis of generativity is the central crisis of parenthood. It relates primarily to the establishment and guidance of the future generation. Parents find their mature fulfillment in the combination of their personalities and energies for the production and care of common offspring. The term *generativity* is employed by Erikson to connote sexual genitality, and in this sense is more specific than other terms such as creativity, productivity, or parenthood. However, Erikson feels that there are some individuals who, because of special and genuine gifts in other directions and for high motives, do not express their generative drive in parenthood, but in other forms of altruistic concern and creativity which absorb their kind of parental responsibility.[1]

Central to the crisis of generativity, whatever the mode of life of the individual, is the development of the capacity for selfless surrender of one's personality and energies. In married life this surrender is to one's partner. In religious life it is to Christ, and ultimately to all mankind. Development of such a capacity is the central problem of this stage in the growth of the healthy personality.

[1] Erik H. Erikson, *Identity and the Life Cycle* (New York: International University Press, 1959), p. 97. The author wishes to express his gratitude to the Editor of the *Review for Religious* for allowing him to reprint in this chapter certain material which first appeared in that publication.

Where such enrichment fails, there may be a regression from generativity to an obsessive need for pseudo-intimacy or extreme and unhealthy self-indulgence. The individual converts his latent love for a partner in marriage and for offspring into a narcissistic self-love. The risk of the generative crisis is a generalized egoism and interpersonal impoverishment.

Psychoanalysts have repeatedly contended that the natural state of man, and the one toward which his previous development leads, is marriage. This is not contrary to Christian tradition, as recent writers on the theology of marriage point out. The individual who is raised lovingly, whose own love is cultivated and brought carefully to maturation, becomes capable of healthy, adult love. The aim and final goal of his evolution is—on the merely natural plane—the complete actualization of his personality in an affective union with an adult of the opposite sex. To be capable of such union is the mark of mature adulthood. To be able to give oneself to another is the prerogative of the person who has terminated the developmental processes of childhood and adolescence successfully.[2]

This is not to imply, of course, that the mere fact of entering upon married life and having children ensures the fullness of personal maturity. Marriage itself is not a psychological necessity. It is rather the capacity for marriage and for all that marriage requires of a person which indicates successful psychological development. The religious man must possess this capacity and must have achieved the level of maturity requisite for marriage. His chastity must not conceal a natural inadequacy.

But within the religious life it is impossible for the religious man to experience marital or parental love. These

[2] Charles B. Trundle, S.J., "Love and Perfect Chastity," *Review for Religious,* 21 (1962), p. 33.

he has freely surrendered, and with them the responsibility
and suffering inherent in parenthood. Charles Peguy wrote
that those who have not had a sick child do not know
what sickness is, and those who have not seen their child
dead do not know what death is. Somehow, the religious
man must acquire the sense of maturity that experiences
such as these—the experiences of raising a family—bring to
a man's personality. Again, it is a question of elevation, of
sublimation.

Like the crisis of intimacy, the crisis of generativity is
problematic to the religious man's chastity. But unlike the
crisis of intimacy, which also involves ultimately the religious man's spirit of poverty, the crisis of generativity is
problematic to the religious man's vow of obedience. These
two aspects of the crisis of generativity demand two radically different solutions—one concerned with the sublimation and supernaturalizing of sexual energies, the other concerned with the elevation of aggressive energies.

The religious man who has vowed himself to a life of
chastity will discover that the perfection of the vow makes
different demands on him at different stages of his mature
development. The chastity of the young adult of twenty-five
is not the same as the chastity of the man of forty. His
physiological state, his psychological and emotional condition change considerably at different stages in his development. At twenty, there is a strong, urgent need for intimate
dealings with others. The young man feels a spontaneous
desire to relate his sentiments and feelings with those of
another person. The man of thirty feels the need for more
reflective companionship, for the expansion of his own personality in unison with that of another person. At forty,
there is a new urgency, as man realizes that his life-giving
powers are undergoing diminution, to see something of

one's self in other beings. The demands of chastity differ at each stage. The renunciation involves at successive stages the satisfaction of having a partner in love, of having a home and family, of being a parent.[3]

In the strength of parenthood, man can discover the most enduring and constant patience, a consistent self-forgetfulness, and a deep and abiding spirit of sacrifice and love. These qualities, as specifically required by the married state, are also renounced when an individual vows religious chastity. For many persons these, and the sense of responsibility parenthood engenders, constitute the most difficult renunciation.

But the call of Christ cannot terminate in a diminution of manhood. The renunciations which the vow requires of the religious man must lead eventually to greater personal enrichment. This is a fundamental law of spiritual development. "I have come that they might have life, and have it more abundantly" (John 10:10). If this condition is not fulfilled, if sacrifice does not lead to growth, there is somewhere an admixture of selfishness and pride.

The renunciation at each stage will necessarily be difficult. The religious man will feel that he is surrendering something of great value. Even the force of his love for Christ will not remove a certain sense of regret. This will differ greatly in different individuals, but the most spiritual of men will find the renunciation difficult at times.

Yet the man of God realizes that Christ's call is a call to a higher and more perfect state. Christ has chosen him to share in a special way His own love. At each critical stage in his development, the religious man will be asked to renew and deepen his love. At each point in the process of his growth, a new and more mature aspect of his love of Christ will be revealed. Each time there will be a choice to make.

[3] Voillaume, *op. cit.*, p. 328.

He will have to choose Christ again—in the crisis of identity, in that of intimacy, generativity, and finally integrity.

The choice during the crisis of generativity is a choice of Christ over against the joys and sorrows, the maturing experiences, of parenthood. The choice of a chaste love for Christ necessitates the sublimation and supernaturalizing of man's desire for procreation. Without such transformation there is impoverishment.

The process whereby sublimation of mature genitality is accomplished in religious life involves a deeper and more penetrating understanding of the love of Christ. More concretely, there must be an extension of one's love to all mankind, especially to those of mankind who are entrusted to the religious man through his apostolic mission. In these he realizes a spiritual parenthood, loving them with the generosity and self-forgetfulness which characterized Christ's love for men.

Such an expansion of one's love does not involve repression, but elevates a natural need to its supernatural fulfillment. There is a constant risk of domineering paternalism and possessiveness. This is avoided only by a universal love which gains expression in each contact with another human being. There is also the risk of a too natural attachment to spiritual children and the desire to see them reflect one's own personal qualities. This in turn is overcome by a love which loves others in Christ and which only seeks Christ's glory. "He must increase, I must decrease" (John 3:30).

Unless such a transformation is accomplished, there will be stagnation. Either the religious man emerges from the crisis of generativity with a more secure and more dedicated love of Christ and the men Christ has given him, or his generosity diminishes and his love deteriorates. There is no halfway. The result of mediocrity is a diminution of chastity. The individual comes to see only the renunciations involved in his choice of Christ. Gradually his love dries up, and he searches for compensation.

As in the intimacy crisis, the risk of the generative crisis to the chastity of the religious man is avoided only by an integral love of Christ. But his personal love of other men must also be integral. Here again it must be marked by such fundamental attitudes as presence, availability, empathy, generosity, fidelity. In this sense the resolution of the intimacy crisis is prerequisite to the resolution of the crisis of generativity, and the resolution of the generativity crisis deepens the individual's sense of intimacy. But the generative crisis also requires resolution of the identity crisis, particularly in the case of the religious man. Only to the extent that the religious man has transformed his own identity into the identity desired of him by Christ, will he supernaturalize his apostolic activity, drawing men to him and ultimately to Christ.

The generative crisis also involves the religious man's obedience. The proper antonym for both generativity and the virtue of obedience is stagnation. If the generative crisis is not resolved, the individual stagnates in the sense of suffering a diminution in human growth. His relations with others lack warmth; his love is constricted; he is irresponsible. If the vow of obedience is not lived in its perfection, there is a stagnation of the same sort, although on a spiritual plane. The individual's obedience is prompted by fear, not love; his behavior lacks purpose; he is irresponsible.

Psychologists have recently pointed out that there is a certain behavioral process of living organisms according to which learned behavior deteriorates over time to more primitive instinctive patterns of activity. This phenomenon the psychologists call an "instinctive drift."

In the practice of virtue a similar process possibly occurs. An act of virtue is a specifically human act and consequently one in which intellect and will play their full parts. Normally, the religious man performs such an act when he initially pledges his life to God on the day of his vows. He acts in a manner specifically human, deliberately and lovingly. His affections are spiritual in nature—directed to a good loved in itself, to God loved in and for Himself.

Yet there is a natural tendency for the fervor and generosity characteristic of his early years to deteriorate and diminish as the religious man is absorbed into the routine of his daily religious life. There is an "instinctive drift" toward mediocrity, often toward a comfortable mediocrity that has been unconsciously rationalized. The spiritual affections become subordinated to the merely sensitive affections, to personal pleasure or utility. The spiritual life vegetates. Energy to transform the sensitive affections into spiritual affections, into a selfless love of God and one's neighbor, decreases.

Such deterioration is inevitable unless there be, with grace, a watchful gathering of strength, a continual self-renewal and self-adaptation. Otherwise the individual is holding fast to a truth which is in the very process of becoming a lie. And the result is a man of incomplete virility, of diminished manhood.

In fact, this diminution follows necessarily from the life of the vows lived poorly. This is the risk all religious men run. There is the risk of becoming in some greater or lesser degree unreliable, closed, self-possessed, miserly—a man damaged by the vow of poverty. There is also the risk of emotional immaturity and subsequent psychological dispersion. Such an individual is energyless and unorganized —his manhood has been damaged by his vow of chastity. And there is the danger of purposelessness, irresponsibility.

There is no inward direction; the individual's life is not consciously and strongly patterned—he has been damaged by his vow of obedience.[4]

The last of these dangers is the one of central interest in discussing the crisis of generativity. Obedience, in the perfection of the virtue, demands a certain spirit of initiative, of purposefulness, of decision. It is antithetical to stagnation. Yet the obedient man risks this stagnation in yielding his will consistently to that of another. He risks mediocrity and spiritual inertia.

One of the fundamental causes of the mediocrity of religious men is spiritual asthenia or inertia. It leads to a lack of a serious and efficacious desire for progress and, consequently, to the surrender of the attempt to cultivate a real interior life. This terminates in a life in which external work and human means predominate, where recollection yields to dissipation of mind. A stunting of religious growth ensues. There is a regression to the natural.

Spiritual asthenia is both a spiritual and psychological problem. It precipitates this migration to mediocrity and brings about the "instinctive drift" that poses a constant threat to spiritual growth. Psychologically, such maladjustment arises in particular from mistaken ascetical notions concerning the nature of certain Christian virtues—among them obedience.

It is said that there are three questions which contemporary Christianity must answer to gain a hearing from modern man. The first question was posed by Spinoza: this is the question of the historical character of the written documents which are the foundations of faith. The second is the question of Marx: it concerns the organization of

[4] John Courtney Murray, S.J., an unpublished conference on the vows, given at Woodstock College, Woodstock, Maryland.

labor, the distribution of goods, and social justice. The
third is Nietzsche's question: whether the values taught by
Christianity, such as gentleness, submission, humility, piety,
have not enfeebled and enervated human nature. Biblical
scholarship and Papal social encyclicals have done much to
supply answers to the first two questions, but little attention
has been paid to the question of Nietzsche.[5]

In fact, any attempt to answer this question is hampered
by a basic deficiency in ascetical vocabulary. There is a
need for terms to denote positively and without their acquired negative connotations such virtues as humility,
meekness, and charity. For every virtue contains an implicit
paradox. Like Christ, the Christian must be submissive and
yet unyielding, gentle and yet demanding, patient and yet
zealous. Often, however, the negative virtues are emphasized, and their positive counterparts are ignored. To express this more generally, ascetical writers often stress the
"meek" virtues and neglect the "assertive" virtues.

St. Thomas, in discussing the moral virtues in relation to
the sensitive appetites, specifies meekness as the virtue cor-
relative to the passion of anger. Although he does not treat
of it, there is perhaps another side to the coin. This is expressed in the virtue, related also to anger, yet something
quite different from meekness, which was exemplified in
the action of our Lord as He drove the money-changers
from the temple. This can perhaps be called "the virtue of
anger" or, without negative connotations, "the virtue of
assertion."

Cultivation of the virtue of assertion is prerequisite to
the perfection of Christian living. It safeguards such virtues
as meekness, patience, and humility from distortion, and

[5] Jean Guitton, *Essays on Human Love* (London: Rockliff, 1951),
pp. 9–10.

serves as a criterion to distinguish the virtue from a psychologically unhealthy counterfeit. In its broadest and most spiritual meaning, assertiveness helps the individual to surmount the problem of spiritual asthenia and inertia and to escape the mediocrity which results from such spiritual stagnation. And for the religious man, the virtue of assertion is closely related to the perfection of his obedience. It is in the tension which he must maintain between a productive assertiveness and a humble and loving submission that the religious man attains to the perfection of his vow and, in this way, successfully terminates his crisis of generativity.

This tension between assertion and submission represents the second aspect of the crisis of generativity in the life of the religious man. The first aspect is concerned with his vow of chastity; and its solution is contained in the sublimation of his capacity for natural, parental love and the transformation of such love into a supernaturalized love for those to whom his apostolic lifework carries him. The second aspect of the generativity crisis relates to obedience, and its solution is contained in the sublimation of the individual's aggressive tendencies and their transformation in the form of assertive and responsible obedience.

In 1922 Sigmund Freud advanced his theory that aggressive behavior is a manifestation of the "death instinct." Freud was strongly impressed by the evidence in World War I of man's aggressive and destructive tendencies. In addition, he had become convinced that not all behavior was explicable in terms of the libido theory. Not all human motivation could be ascribed ultimately to some broad sexual instinct. Therefore he postulated a complementary instinct—the death instinct of destruction and aggression. Since then the concept has received considerable

attention in psychiatric theory and research. It is important
in the present context because there are psychiatrists and
psychologists who feel that the major problems in religious
life originate, not in repressed libidinal impulses, but in
repressed aggression.

In its most general sense, aggression is a fundamental
characteristic of all living organisms. It refers to any ex-
penditure of energy directed at securing what is needed
from the environment. To win and keep friends, to be effective in dealing with people, require an output of energy
and consequently aggressive behavior. To write a play, to
paint a picture, to deliver a message in public, to win ac-
claim—all are acts of aggression, since all require activity
aimed at certain definite results.

Technically, aggression means "going toward" and relates
to a necessary part of the normal growth process. The sentence, "Behold I see him aggress and enter into his own,"
dating to 1575, expresses this broader meaning of the word
aggression. More frequently, however, aggression is used in
its pejorative sense. Hence in Freudian theory, where
aggression has been made the basis of the death instinct,
there is no recognition of the meaning of aggression which
equates it with life.

Consequently, it is necessary to distinguish aggressive
from assertive behavior. Aggression is negatively toned and
refers to behavior that is not called for by the objective
situation. It is directed against one's self or another and is
essentially anti-social in nature. Such behavior involves acts
of going against someone, attacking, disparaging, encroach-
ing, or some other form of hostile behavior.

Assertive behavior, on the other hand, helps the individual to satisfy his needs without harming himself or
others. It is socially beneficial since it brings the individual
to defend himself against attack, provides him with a

stimulus to further himself in his work, and enables him to carry on his work for the goals of his life.

In the young child no distinction is possible between aggressive and assertive behavior. The infant is aroused to action by his physiological needs. His activity is aggressive, but not in the negative sense. Frustration awakens the need to test his capacity to deal with external forces. In this way he gradually discovers the reality boundaries of the organized world into which he is entering.

Gradually the child develops potential for destructive (aggressive) or constructive (assertive) behavior. If he is overprotected or subjected to rigorous autocratic discipline, he may react destructively. The result is socially unacceptable aggressive behavior. This is not tolerated by the child's parents and typically is forcefully suppressed. The outcome is often a strong feeling of insecurity and subsequent social maladjustment and emotional illness. This has two manifestations in adult life, each equally severe: pathological aggression, or over-compliance and over-acquiescence to others. Both of these behavioral manifestations of aggressive tendencies may appear in religious life. Most probably the second occurs more frequently; certainly it is less frequently recognized as a serious neurotic symptom.

If, on the other hand, the child's potential for aggressive behavior is channeled along positive lines, if aggressive behavior is allowed in a socially acceptable form, then this potential is constructively released in assertive behavior by a maturing ego, and the outcome is productive living. This, of course, is a difficult task and is perhaps never perfectly achieved in our culture.

Therapy in extreme cases of aggressive behavior focuses upon patterns of repressed aggression formed in childhood and upon reactivation of the images and memories of earlier experiences in which these defenses were patterned. Once this reactivation is accomplished, the individual attempts to remove the distortions of perception that led him to view the world as a threatening place in which one can survive only by aggression (or over-compliance). In the more "normal" case, aggressive tendencies can be controlled by the exercise of good judgment, self-critical analysis, and the rechanneling of energy into assertive and constructive, rather than aggressive and destructive, behavior. This involves the transformation or sublimation of negative tendencies into the positive patterns of assertive behavior. Such sublimation of aggression is achieved, for example, by the strategy of giving the young child nails and wood so that he hammers these instead of the furniture.

In adult life the dynamics of sublimation are, of course, much more complex than in the case of the child, and differ considerably in differing personalites. Nevertheless, for the religious man it is perhaps generally true that the process of sublimation is carried out in reference to an apostolic lifework performed under obedience. Assertion, or the constructive and sublimated expression of the individual's aggressive tendencies, can become in this context an act of virtue and a complement to the perfection of his vow of obedience.

Such assertion also helps him to resolve his crisis of generativity, providing him with an outlet for sublimated creative and productive enterprise. In this way he avoids the dangers of spiritual asthenia and apostolic stagnation.

Stagnation in the psychosocial development of the individual is indicated by several characteristics. Each symptom evidences a failure in growth, a failure on the part of the individual to cope with situations where positive and constructive assertive behavior was necessary. And each is indicative of a failure to resolve successfully the generative crisis.

The first of these characteristics is nonparticipation. The individual maintains a consistent emotional distance from others. He is afraid of close dealings with other people—he asks nothing of them, even in emergencies. On the other hand, he may be quite willing to help others, provided it does not involve him emotionally. He is an onlooker at life, observing a drama acted on a stage—a drama which is not too exciting or interesting, and for the most part rather dull.

Allied to this is an attitude of resignation. The individual believes that it is better not to nourish high hopes. A restriction is placed on aspirations; a pessimistic outlook develops. The individual may vaguely and idly desire certain objects, but this does not generate a concrete, enthusiastic activity toward the objects desired. There is a resistance to change, to anything new. The individual is convinced that he is caught in a rut and that it is now too late to escape.

Concomitantly, there is a lack of serious striving for personal achievement, an aversion to effort. The individual consciously or unconsciously rejects both achievement and effort. He minimizes his talents or denies them flatly. He resents exhortation. There is a total lack of confidence and, subsequently, inertia. The individual is listless, ineffective, and often neurasthenic. Inspirations may come, but energy to achieve is lacking.

Finally, the individual lacks a sense of purpose. Even within his vocation he is uncertain of what he wants to do with his life. Tasks are engaged and surrendered sporadically. There are long periods of doubt and uncertainty. The individual is often incapable of even minor decisions. His main objective seems to be to avoid life's conflicts completely. He seeks and then holds rigidly to oversimplified solutions to his problems.

This is the syndrome of stagnation. It typifies the individual who is apathetically mediocre in his religious life —and hence a failure. For Christ required assertive enthusiasm of His followers: "The kingdom of heaven suffers violence, and the violent bear it away" (Matt. 11:12).

In general, the danger of stagnation is avoided through exercise of patterns of behavior diametrically opposed to those just mentioned. The individual must assert himself by going out to others, by being available to them. He must strive to participate fully in the joint enterprise of humanization, and cultivate a fundamental optimism, a joy in the Good News of the Christian message. Finally, he must develop a zealous and mature sense of responsibility and a steady purposiveness.

More specifically, the life of religious obedience offers two avenues for sublimated and successful assertion—not of course implying undue aggression or ambition, but rather constructive and therefore "generative" activity. The first brings the individual to a realistic view of his personal capacities. In line with this, it is possible secondly for the individual to assert himself apostolically in a spirit of committed dedication.

Perhaps the highest homage to truth is the ability to recognize one's own personal limitations.[6] This is not achieved easily. The necessary experimentation involves the possibility of frequent failure. But the individual must advance confidently, endeavoring to use his gifts to their maximum. This is precisely the point of our Lord's parable of the talents. The man who has built castles in the air has not labored in vain. They are where they should be. The crucial

[6] John LaFarge, S.J., *An American Amen* (New York: Farrar, Straus, and Cudahy, 1958), p. 208.

question is whether he can build the foundations under them. Perhaps he cannot; but perhaps he can. At least he must try, by experimentation, to gain adequate and accurate knowledge of his ability.

Religious obedience, of course, controls and sets limits to the boundary of an individual's activity. Nevertheless it is necessary for the individual to assert the requisite initiative, obediently and prayerfully. The superior should, when this is possible, allow such experimentation, even though it is much easier to enforce rigidly a uniformity of behavior which permits no exceptions. Rigidity of operation suffocates initiative and seems to express a spirit antithetical to that of our Lord who came "to cast fire upon the earth" (Luke 12:49). Admittedly, it is difficult in a large religious organization to maintain perfectly the urgency and freedom of the Gospel. This is the risk run by an efficient bureaucracy.

On the other hand, the individual who is appointed president of a college or university must have no doubts about his ability. The necessary self-knowledge will certainly be lacking, however, if he has been shielded from responsibility for many years prior to his appointment. God does not operate against nature. He will not bestow a miraculous grace-of-office where no natural means have been taken to insure that the individual is prepared for the job to which he is assigned. Absolutely essential to this preparation is the opportunity to determine accurately what one is capable of achieving.

Then second, given adequate self-knowledge, the individual must always be aiming higher. There is the constant danger that apostolic dedication, whatever specific work it involves, may be incomplete, something short of total. This may be the result of the security of the religious life, or it may be the product of minimization of the value of competition. For the religious life offers a kind of intimacy and an ideal of equality that tends to disregard the American value of competition. The competitive struggle among career men, which supposedly provides an incentive to hard work and successful achievement, is deliberately played down in the religious life. To the extent that it is not replaced by other motives and incentives, there may result a relaxation of demands for laborious efforts and high performance.[7]

Whatever the precise reason, although the religious man may live a very full and active day, it is still possible to ask whether he is operating at top capacity. If an efficiency expert, such as is employed in industry, were to make a time-study of American religious men and women, he would probably show them how to increase greatly their effectiveness. But this would still be on the merely natural level. Apostolic dedication has another and more important side to it.

For ultimately the fruit of the apostolate is proportioned to dedication to the work of Christ, the corollary of which is total dedication to personal holiness. The religious man proclaims Christ most perfectly by the dynamic apologetic of sanctity. This is the only unanswerable argument. The most important task, then, is that of increasing supernatural effectiveness. This requires not more activity, but less. It requires enthusiastic and energetic cultivation of a prayerful attitude, of an active capacity for stillness. Man is, as Rilke said, a great waster of sorrows. Perhaps the individual in religious life offends God more by sins of omission than in any other way. To fail to bear witness to the spiritual, to a spirit of recollection which orientates the sorrows, sufferings, and joys of life to God's glory—to fail here mani-

---

[7] Fichter, *op. cit.*, p. 208.

fests a partial religious dedication, a dedication necessarily incomplete.

The acquisition of a realistic knowledge of personal ability and total, committed dedication to one's apostolate offer two means of assertive behavior which guarantee that the religious man's obedience is responsible and mature. In this way they serve as avenues for productive and creative activity and as criteria for the resolution of the psychological crisis of generativity. But it is unsatisfactory merely to restrict discussion to the natural, psychological side. An individual may be naturally assertive, enthusiastic, and energetic—and not at all virtuous. Hence it is necessary to distinguish natural endowments from virtue, psychological maturity from spiritual maturity. The natural possibly facilitates the supernatural process, but there can be psychological maturity where there is theological immaturity. On the other hand, a person can live in the presence of God and perform virtuous actions while at the same time manifesting a certain psychological infantilism indicative of a defect in human development rather than of a lack of response to God's grace.

In the performance of any act of virtue there must be a direction of the intellect and will to God. The action which is merely the product of natural temperament cannot be an act of virtue. This leads to two considerations—the first dealing with "the virtue of assertion," the second with the virtue of obedience.

The individual who is able to defend his opinion in an argument, to refute an unwarranted accusation, insinuation, or imposition, to remonstrate against neglect or injustice, to refuse a request or an offer that he feels he should not grant or accept—such an individual is not behaving uncharitably. He is merely displaying the normal signs of a healthy self-assertion. Such an individual is capable of feeling and expressing criticism and of acting energetically without undue emotional strain. There is a relative freedom from diffuse unconscious hostility and a comparatively secure self-esteem. When such behavior is directed toward God's glory and the good of souls, and when it is performed within the bounds of obedience, it is virtuous and pleasing in God's sight.

This possibly contradicts certain traditional and facile formulas which dictate that such behavior as criticism of others or refusal to perform elicited acts of charity is necessarily and in every case morally wrong. But it does not contradict the action of Christ, particularly of Christ remonstrating with the Pharisees or driving the money-changers from the temple. Nor does it contradict the action of the saint who, like Christ, lives at the limit of his powers. In a sense the saint surrenders to his human nature, but only to derive from this source a fulfilling and virile enthusiasm and zeal. Instead of fighting against his natural impulses, the saint directs them all to his ultimate end. In this way he achieves the triumph of an integral manhood.

Yet there is always the possibility of self-deception. To be virtuous, assertive behavior must transcend the merely natural and must arise out of the deliberate and free choice of God and His will. The individual must be sensitive to the operation of God's grace and open to His inspiration. Here the religious man has, besides spiritual direction, the norm of obedience.

St. Augustine said that we need only love and then do as we wish. For love wants only what the beloved wants. Beginning in love, obedience terminates in love. The first act of love is a committal. All subsequent acts of obedience merely extend this initial commitment to the will of God.

In this way the individual transcends himself and gives

himself over to something greater than himself. Silently he obeys and unquestioningly. For the will of Christ is seen to be mirrored in the will of the superior. The obedient man submits himself to serve a demand he did not invent, to serve Reality. In their perfection his actions have a child-like quality about them, but they are even more similar to the actions of fully developed manhood.

Yet there is the possibility of self-deception here as well. Obedience may conceal the basic weakness of an individual who has not attained full independence and is afraid of freedom of thought and action. Or it may conceal the weakness of a man who is pained by the slightest disagreement with others and quickly submits to the will of others to maintain the security of peace and agreement. In this sense obedience is not virtuous, but characterizes the insecure, compliant, perhaps neurotic, individual.

Consequently there must be a lived tension, a delicate balance achieved beteeen obedience and assertion. There should be room for personal initiative, for freedom of action, responsibility, and experimentation. On the other hand, there must be a consistent recognition that what is involved is God's work and that God's ways are not man's ways. Performed under obedience, the actions of the religious man must be marked by an energetic and enthusiastic love, even should these actions be performed under conditions which seemingly debilitate and stifle personal development.

The mind of Christ, apprehended truly in His Church and, subsequently, through the Church's authority, in religious superiors, directs to fullness human motives, desires, ambitions, talents. The quest for the apprehension of Christ's will is directed by love and results in the perception that difficult and crucial decisions no longer need be resolved by merely natural means. Rather they are assumed into the structure of grace. This in no way lessens the tension, but it situates the struggle. Now there is the realized presence of God.

The last word of love is simply service—service marked by the solicitude of sons of the Church. This solicitude elicits zeal—not a restless but a restful zeal, which holds suspect any easy triumph which removes the sense of mystery. For Reality is mysterious. The expansion of man through the life of grace is known only to the Father. Man labors in the face of this mystery while awaiting its revelation.

There is, then, a point of mystery at which assertiveness and obedient submission tend to merge. The action of the individual is one action, directed by man to its goal, yet conditioned by the Divine Will. The paradox of the apostolic mind involves a paradox basic to Christianity because it was basic to the personality of Christ. For Christ was man, meek and humble of heart, and yet a man whose words and deeds prompted men to marvel: "For He was teaching them as one having authority and not as their Scribes and Pharisees" (Matt. 7:29).

In summary, the crisis of generativity occurs in two distinct forms in the life of the religious man. The first aspect of the crisis is that which relates specifically to religious chastity. Here failure to resolve the crisis of generativity results in personal impoverishment and inability to interact with other human beings with warmth and affection. The individual in religious life risks becoming, psychologically, a "confirmed bachelor."

Consequently, there must be sublimation of parental affection through a rechanneling of such affection in the form of legitimate apostolic love and concern for those committed to one's spiritual care. This involves certain risks, but is achieved when the individual's love for Christ has supernaturalized natural, human love.

The second aspect of the crisis of generativity is that which relates specifically to religious obedience. Here failure to achieve a successful resolution results in apostolic stagnation and irresponsibility. The perfection of obedience requires productive, creative, and, in this sense, generative activity.

Consequently, the virtue of obedience requires the exercise of the virtue of assertion. In this way sublimation of potentially detrimental aggressive tendencies is achieved in mature, responsible, and supernaturalized assertiveness. This requires a delicate tension between assertion and submission within the context of the vow of obedience.

Integrity

The final crisis in the life cycle and the summation of all that went before is what Erikson has called the integrity crisis. Previously, the adult person has faced and resolved the crisis of his identity. He has learned to be concerned with other people, to interact intimately with them. And he has been in some way the exemplar for others and the generator of things and ideas. Now he must resolve the crisis inherent in the formation of a personally significant and meaningful "life style" or philosophy of life.

The danger of failure to resolve this crisis is subsequent lack of ego integration and perhaps despair. There may be an unconscious terror of death and a feeling that time is short—too short to begin again a life that is regretted and meaningless. Often such despair is hidden behind a show of disgust, of chronic contempt for particular institutions and people. But this disgust and contempt is merely indicative of the individual's latent contempt for himself.

Successful resolution of the integrity crisis is manifested in the attitudes a person displays. He accepts himself and the particular style of life he has chosen without regret, and with a certain joy and peace. There is also an acceptance of other people and of the modes of life they have chosen. Other styles of life and the whole history of civilization are respected. The insights and outlooks of other ages are admired, and their contributions to man's historical

108

and cultural development are received appreciatively and assimilated with necessary modification into one's own life style. Although aware of the value and dignity of other life styles, the man who has resolved the integrity crisis is prepared to defend the value and dignity of his own life style against physical and social encroachment. He is convinced of his own truth, and without this truth life is for him a meaningless absurdity.

Many adults, however, never attain this level of maturity. They never resolve the integrity crisis, and spend their lives in a restless flight from meaninglessness. Perhaps the social conditions of contemporary life exaggerate and heighten this tension. In fact, it has been said that despair is the only attitude possible to a generation of men and women who were born near the beginning of the First World War, who reached the age of twenty as Hitler was seizing power in Germany, who completed their education during the Second World War, and who today must see their children and their works mature in a world threatened with instantaneous nuclear destruction.[1]

Where it does not attain the pitch of despair, there is a sense of generalized boredom. The individual who has not successfully resolved the crisis of integrity feels that he is not attached to what he is doing, to what he is. He is bored with living with himself, and has grown weary of chasing after elusive distractions. He desires to be compensated in some way, yet he does not know how he is to fill in time. He has let himself down. In his boredom he has become hypnotized by the slow and steady beat of empty time.

Modern European philosophers have formulated the

[1] Albert Camus, in his Nobel Prize acceptance speech, December, 1957. The author wishes to express his gratitude to the Editor of the *Review for Religious* for allowing him to reprint in this chapter certain material which first appeared in that publication.

philosophy of despair, reflecting the inability of man to resolve the crisis of integrity. The fundamental presupposition of such a philosophy is that man's dignity consists in the realization that he exists in a world of material things, and that there is nothing beyond. The universe is meaningless and godless. The condition of man is essentially pitiful. For Heidegger, man is "stretched toward death," in excruciating anguish. For Sartre, he is a "useless passion," a superfluous excrescence fit only to provoke nausea. For Jaspers, he is bound in a tragic quest for an infinite God whom his finite situation will never permit him to attain.

In America, a fundamental, indigenous optimism colors, even eradicates, despair. In the face of a life that is utterly incomprehensible, contemporary American society has evolved two secularistic philosophies. Both of these are false and necessarily un-Christian. Yet many individuals find that one or the other of these provides a personally satisfying answer to the question of life. As philosophies of optimism, they achieve their primary aim in counteracting the despair of meaninglessness. The first of these philosophies of life is that of scientific secularism.

The adherents to such a philosophy are respectable, intelligent, cultured, dedicated to the material welfare of the secular community as the highest human good. This dedication is frequently religious in character—ordered to the religion of scientism which replaces God with the idols of Science and Progress. Christianity is admitted to the modern forum condescendingly, and with marked reservations. "Now when they heard of a resurrection of the dead, some began to sneer, but others said, 'We will hear you again on this matter'" (Acts 17:32). The "modern pagan," like the Athenian in St. Paul's audience, displays contempt or, at best, an indulgent curiosity when confronted with the

Christian message. Only science is considered to make meaningful statements about life and the universe. Its dogmas are accepted without reservation.

The apostles of the religion of scientism are the intellectual elite of American culture—schoolteachers, college professors, scientists, engineers, physicians. They disseminate their gospel in the classroom, primarily by ruling out all discussion of God and religion. Since God cannot be discussed scientifically and demonstrated experimentally, the question of His existence is a meaningless question and is only answered by silence. Many students come to accept this agnosticism, though they outwardly retain their religious practices. God is never mentioned in many homes, and at church, when He is mentioned, it is often in the asthenic tones of a hygienic, sugar-coated parody of Christianity. In fact, it has become impolite to mention God. Modern man fears to offend people by mentioning God and religion. It is better not to speak of such topics.

In this way scientific secularism, as a philosophy of life and a pseudo-religion, deadens the religious sensitivities of contemporary man. Truth is relative to empirical evidence and is attained only through experimental procedures. God is excluded on principle, and the ultimate end of man is the material welfare of the human community.

This degenerates into the second form of secularism characteristic of contemporary American society—suburban secularism. In this country one-third of the population, roughly sixty million people, live in suburbia. Their philosophy of life, in many cases, predicates as ultimates comfort and success. Again dedication becomes almost religious, and Comfort and Success become idols of worship. In his devotion to these idols, the suburban status-seeker restlessly pursues prestige symbols—newer power mowers, cars, and automatic dishwashers. He is other-directed, a conformist, whose central concern on a weekend may be working in his flower-garden. No one cares, one sociologist noted, whether a person believes in God, but he had better cut his grass.

In the scramble for success and its prestige symbols, other more important values are often ignored. The family is divided since the father is kept busy at the office and typically is home only on Sunday. Religion is a once-a-week affair, of primarily social importance. Trivialities occupy time and attention. One poll showed that the issue of central importance for the people of an average community was the complaint that too many dogs were running unleashed on lawns.

Science and suburban living are not, of course, necessarily evil. But scientism and suburban secularism, as philosophies of life, are intellectually and morally deleterious. They threaten seriously the religious sensitivities of modern man, forcing upon him attitudes of mind which are essentially materialistic and a-religious. Consequently, they endanger religious growth and the eventual appearance of a fully Christocentric and integrated personality.

Constantly beleaguered by the message of the gospel of secularism, the religious man, like the modern man of contemporary society, finds it increasingly difficult to live by the Gospel of Christ. His attitudes tend to become colored by the attitudes of the culture around him, and he often seems to regress in his evaluations to a secular standard which measures success in materialistic units. The teacher often tends to favor the child who comes from the "nice" home, or the pastor speaks highly of a "nice" family (where "nice" is defined more by material goods and success than by true Christian love).

And, insofar as religious life is primarily a life of the vows, this infiltration of naturalistic attitudes into religious ideals hits at the very core of the life of the religious man.

Poverty is vowed by a simple act of the will, but requires vigilance and sacrifice in every detail of one's life. The virtue of poverty demands, for example, that the individual be scrupulous in the use of his time, as if his livelihood depended on it. Too often, however, the individual tends to take certain things for granted, and becomes complacent in his poverty. He develops the attitude that what is given to him is the just recompense for his labors, thereby losing the sense of dependency proper to a poor man who relies upon the kindness and generosity of others. In other words, his attitude tends to become quite "natural." The individual may also find an increasing tendency to salvage as much sensual pleasure as possible (short of sin) from books, papers, movies, and other forms of entertainment. Self-discipline in thought and imagination, and the use of penance, may become increasingly difficult to practice. Gradually the virtue of chastity becomes negative, anemic, and almost unbearable. Obedience may be undermined by a spirit of criticism which, although perhaps deriving from complaints that are entirely true and justifiable, is primarily negative in character and makes no reference to the supernatural. At every point, in all of his attitudes, religious man encounters the threat of a gradual migration to the natural.

Yet growth in the spiritual life consists simply in extending the supernatural into the realm of the natural so that it permeates life. The only access to God is personal and active commitment. In this way the thoughts of God become gradually assimilated, until there is no evaluation, no decision, no thought which does not have its roots in God. For it is only from the light which streams constantly from heaven, as Simone Weil once wrote, that a tree derives the energy to strike its roots deep into the soil. In fact, the tree is rooted in the sky.

This, then, is the risk run by the religious man in the resolution of his integrity crisis. Once the novelty and fervor of the early years of religious life have abated, there is the constant danger of a regression to the natural. This is intensified by contact with a culture which is founded upon secularistic principles and devoted to secularistic goals. The pressures this culture exerts may be unnoticeable, but they are not innocuous.

If the religious man is to surmount these difficulties and defend himself against the pressures of a secularistic society, he must be certain of the value and dignity of his own life style. He must excise through an initial act of decision—one continually renewed—the mentality of a naturalistic secularism, scientific or suburban.

But secularism is only one of the forces which aggravate the integrity crisis of the religious man. It is an external force—external to the religious community. There is also an internal force which often operates to the detriment of the spiritual growth of the individual—a force within the religious community. This necessitates a discussion of conformity pressures in religious life, and their effects upon the ideals and growth of the individual member of the community.

Many of the studies of social psychology—especially in recent years—have been concerned with the investigation of conformity behavior. This research and subsequent theoretical explanations have done much to clarify the precise nature of the various influences involved in bringing an individual to conform to group norms. It will perhaps prove helpful to briefly discuss some of these influences and their effects on the individual's behavior.

The group enforces norms of behavior so that it can control the responses of its members. This is especially important for the smooth functioning of large groups. To effect this conformity, the group must (1) state a rule, (2) maintain surveillance over its members, and (3) apply sanctions.[2] Initially, there must be external enforcement. Ultimately, it is intended that the individual internalize these norms and apply them to himself without the necessity of external enforcement.

In order that the group may effect such conformity, it is important that accurate communication of norms be possible, especially when a norm involves complex patterns of behavior. Similarly, for group surveillance to be effective, the behavior of each individual must be identifiable. For sanctions to be applied, the group must be able to control the fate of the members in some way. The greater the dependence of the members on the group, the greater the power the group exerts over them.

Research has indicated that conformity is greatest when an individual is highly attracted to the group, when he is a newcomer to the group, or when he is minimally accepted by other members of the group. Nonconformity is determined by the individual's ability to escape exposure to the rule or, when he cannot do this, to misinterpret it. Typically, this strategy is unrealistic, and the individual must avoid conformity either by avoiding surveillance or by acquiring a value to the group so that he can counteract the group's power. But if it is healthy and if it is to succeed, nonconformity must originate in strong personal convictions.

Conformity pressures may be applied in various ways, and their effects upon the individual will vary accordingly. The group may, for example, enforce its norms by surveillance of the individual members. It punishes severely

[2] John W. Thibaut and Harold H. Kelley, *The Social Psychology of Groups* (New York: Wiley, 1959), pp. 240–241.

all nonconformity. In this case, public compliance is the most general and dependable consequence. Such compliance is non-voluntary, and therefore the norm is not internalized by the individual.

Second, the group may apply only positive sanctions (rewarding conformity, but not punishing nonconformity). Surveillance is not rigidly enforced. The only necessary condition is some consistency in rewarding proper behavior. If this condition is fulfilled, the individual begins to accept the proper behavior as autonomously rewarding. He identifies with the group and comes to value what the group values. Consensus forms; norms emerge; rôle relationships are established.

Finally, there is the situation in which the individual obtains his reward, not directly from the group, but from satisfactory fulfillment of the task. The group functions in this instance to assist the individual in accomplishing the task successfully. The effect of the group is dependent upon the perceived validity and reliability of the information given and upon the assistance rendered the individual. Group surveillance is not necessary. The individual derives from the group useful "content," which he assimilates or internalizes in the accomplishment of the task at hand.

These three processes of social pressure—punishment, positive sanction, and information and assistance—and their effects upon the individual—his compliance, identification, or internalization—may be analytically distinguished, but typically they interact in any concrete situation. There are usually positive rewards involved in conforming to group expectations, negative forms of punishment if the individual is consistently recalcitrant, and subsequently internalization of group norms.

Within the context of the religious life, it is helpful to

distinguish between a healthy and an unhealthy conformity. In one sense, conformity has positive value. St. Paul admonished his Christians to be of the same mind (Phil. 3:16). It is this healthy conformity which dictates that the religious man conform to the spirit of his institute. The religious community will state certain norms, maintain surveillance—especially in the initial phases of training—and apply necessary positive and negative sanctions. Gradually, it is hoped that the individual will internalize these norms —not merely complying or identifying with the actions of those around him, but making the norms and ideals of the institute his own.

This healthy conformity to the spirit of the institute, however, often requires a healthy independence and nonconformity to the attitudes and practices of "the crowd." The spirit of the crowd is equivalently the spirit of a few vociferous individuals of inferior religious ideals. These individuals are not malicious; they simply do not possess the high ideals of others. Surreptitiously, they undermine the convictions of others by showing their disapproval in indirect ways. Their influence spreads—primarily because so many members of the religious community possess a false, passive concept of charity. Ultimately, the group appears to think as the individuals with the lowest ideals think.

This poses a serious threat to the ego integrity and personal convictions of the religious man. Studies by social psychologists on "reference group theory" have shown that, typically, if a man stands alone, or seems to stand alone, in holding something dear or in despising some good that others cherish, he not only suffers a loss of status; he is not likely to continue holding his beliefs with much conviction. Similarly, there is considerable evidence that norms induced by a strong subgroup may have a great deal more

motivating force than those induced by the organization as
a whole.[3] In religious life the subgroup may, in the most
extreme instance, operate to effect rather serious deviations
from the norms and ideals of the institute. More often such
a group enforces a generalized mediocrity. Perhaps the
motivation of the individuals constituting this subgroup
derives from an unconscious guilt generated by their own
inability to achieve their religious ideals, with the consequent desire, again unconscious, to prevent others from
succeeding where they had failed. The success of others in
attaining their religious ideals threatens to aggravate, even
to bring to consciousness, their own feelings of guilt.

Since they lack numerical superiority, the individuals
who generate the "crowd spirit" must compensate in some
other way. Their influence is disproportionate to their
numbers mainly because of the domineering character of
their personalities. They enforce conformity in the same
manner as other groups: stating rules, maintaining surveillance, and applying sanctions. But because of the force-
ful, although necessarily indirect, manner in which they
show disapproval of certain practices, they exert a considerable influence on the newcomer or on the individual
who feels that he is not accepted by the other members of
the religious community. Consequently, this small subgroup
is able to perpetrate the illusion that their norms and practices are those of the community as a whole. They draw
unsure and unreflective individuals to their own side. Subsequently, there is a general leveling off of religious spirit,
and some individuals lose or fail to actualize their high
ideals.

One particular rule of behavior dictated by "the crowd"

[3] Lester Coch and John R. French, "Overcoming Resistance to
Change," *Human Relations*, 1 (1948), 520.

presents a special danger to the resolution of the integrity crisis of the religious man. Basically, the problem concerns a typically irrational fear of "hypocrisy."

Perhaps "the foulmouthed saint," Holden Caulfield, of J. D. Salinger's novel, *The Catcher in the Rye*, best exemplifies the irrational antipathy for hypocrisy or "phoniness" which is extremely prevalent in American culture. The reason for this fear of hypocrisy is not entirely understood. Most probably it results from a tendency to develop oversimplified, black and white ethical norms in a society where values are uncertain and where cultural discontinuities often preclude adequate moral maturity. One of the consequences of this fear of phoniness is an irrational fear of displaying one's religion. Americans hate to wear their religion on their sleeve and consequently often do not wear it at all.

Such a fear produces the "Bing Crosby-type priest" who is a hail fellow well met, or the individual in religious life who is a "good guy." (This means, "You would hardly know that he is a member of a religious order.") The "crowd" argues that the best thing to do is to be "normal," to act "naturally." Yet St. Ignatius of Loyola regarded external edification as the most important form of apostolate of the Society of Jesus, taking precedence over prayers and even over the Mass, the administration of the sacraments, and preaching. Max Schleer once wrote that there is nothing in the world that attracts a person toward good so forcibly, so immediately, and so inevitably as the spectacle of a good man doing good.

But the "crowd" condemns those who emphasize externals (admittedly there is nothing quite as exasperating as the individual who takes a second longer to genuflect or who strikes his breast repeatedly as he prays). It propagates the mistaken notion of American culture that a man

is a hypocrite, a "phony," if he expresses outwardly what
he does not feel inwardly. There is, of course, the problem
of unfortunate exaggerations and "piety for piety's sake."
Yet it is highly unsatisfactory for the religious man to react
to pietism by never manifesting piety. This reaction frequently produces a general reluctance to speak of spiritual
topics and an ostentatious infringement of certain "non-
essential" rules—especially silence.

It is interesting to note, however, that an external action
—no matter what the concomitant internal state may be
initially—can have the psychological effect of generating an
identical inner attitude. This "actional identification,"
whereby the outward action (for example, kneeling in worship) brings about an inward attitude (of interior submission perhaps), has always been insisted upon by spiritual
writers—particularly when speaking of the acts preliminary to prayer. The same psychological effect can result
from the suspension of feeling—from acting "hypo-
critically" or "unauthentically"—in situations where edification and good example are called for. The ultimate aim
is to act on principle; rationally and deliberately, rather
than on feeling. External silence is of little spiritual value
if it originates in boredom or melancholy. It should be the
result of a personally meaningful choice.

The goal of religious transformation is the possession of
that mind which was in Christ Jesus (Phil. 2:5). Yet as the
religious man comes in contact with the channels of God's
grace, gaining confidence and strength in his spiritual commitment, he frequently finds that there are psychological
obstacles and deeply rooted attitudes preventing the fully
rational and free expression of personal decision which
normally provides the basis for the higher achievements of

supernatural life. Spiritual directors are coming to realize that faith is strongest in an integrated, well-adjusted, emotionally healthy individual. The person who comes to understand the previously unknown and unconscious sources of his motivation is more free and responsible and, consequently, capable of higher sanctity.[4]

Aside from serious psychological difficulties, such as neurotic habits, compulsions, or severe depression (which may require psychiatric treatment), regression to a naturalistic mentality through contact with the external, secularistic modern world and the decline of spiritual fervor resulting from sources of conformity pressure within the religious community constitute the most subtle and pervasive obstacles to religious transformation and complete ego integrity. To counteract the infiltration of materialistic secularism and to withstand the leveling influence of the "crowd spirit" within the religious community, the individual must constantly re-examine his own semi-conscious patterns of thought. For it is at this semi-conscious level that gradual migration to the natural occurs.

The study of man's cognitive activity is today a topic of intense experimental investigation in scientific psychology. In the present context, it is perhaps advantageous to consider briefly a few of the implications of this area of psychology for understanding certain of the processes involved in religious growth. Specifically, since the forces mentioned above militate against the attainment of a fully mature and integral life style, it should prove helpful to examine how it is that cognitive processes deleterious to religious growth develop, and how they may be counteracted.

It is important, first of all, to recognize what it is that the

[4] George Hagmaier and Robert W. Gleason, *Counselling the Catholic* (New York: Sheed and Ward, 1959), p. 247.

psychologist is referring to when he speaks of cognitive activity. Man's intellect is not a material power; and, since the experimental psychologist is restricted in his observations to the activities of a psychophysiological organism, the activity with which he is concerned is not intellection as such, but rather a process preliminary to and less perfect than the activity of the intellect. He is concerned with a mental and perhaps neural state which has been organized through past experience, and which exerts a directive influence on the individual's habitual responses to a certain combination of objects or to a given situation. The psychologist is not concerned with whether the activity he investigates is conscious. Typically it is unconscious—that is, not immediately susceptible to introspected report—and this can be an advantage and a danger.

Such cognitions, frequently unrecognized, can exert great influence upon an individual's patterns of behavior. In the terminology of scientific psychology, a person unconsciously forms "coding systems"[5] (ways of grouping and relating information about the environment). Such systems are constantly subject to change and reorganization, facilitate new learning, and are themselves the products of learning. Several of the conditions under which coding systems are acquired are relevant here, principally the rôle of past experience and the motivational factors which influence coding systems.

The degree to which newly acquired knowledge is patterned can be influenced temporarily by situational instructions or, more permanently, by past experience. Obviously, the most important factor is past experience. By living in a certain professional or social setting, the individual

[5] Jerome S. Bruner, "'Going beyond the Information Given," *Contemporary Approaches to Cognition* (Cambridge: Harvard Univer. Press, 1957), p. 49.

learns to approach a new experience along definite lines—
to develop a professional frame of reference with respect
to coding events. The mathematician, the housewife, and
the truck driver have their own particular frames of reference. And the religious man also gradually tends to develop certain modes of coding events, certain patterns of
thought, which are uniquely his. To learn to live in a setting which is pre-eminently supernatural and to see events
within a spiritual frame of reference is, of course, a complex and difficult process. It requires deliberate cultivation
of spiritual habits and eradication of unspiritual habits.
Above all, there is need of continually renewed motivation.

An impelling motivational state affects the extent to
which a person is able to acquire and stabilize cognitive
patterns. Obviously, the more unnatural (super-natural)
these patterns of thought, the more motivation required. If
faith is to live, wrote Newman, it must love. This necessarily implies an enthusiastic and loving, personal encounter, through grace, with Christ, who is the perfect
model of man living and thinking as God wills him, His
soul and body resplendent with God's own mind and love
and splendor.

This love is not necessarily an emotional and consciously
fervent love. For many persons it happens that the more
they love God, the less this love is experienced emotionally.
In the service of God feelings are merely of secondary importance. An impelling motivational state does not mean
feeling zealous or emotionally enthusiastic. The enthusiasm
of love has only one criterion: whether or not the will of
God is willed at each moment.

With this caution in mind—that the essence of love is
not feeling, but an orientation of the will—the individual
must constantly renew his motivation for spiritual progress.
Often there is no progress simply because the individual

has no supernatural goals and, consequently, no motivation.
He applies himself to prayer and spiritual exercises and
frequents the sacraments, but he does not advance. He
neither overcomes his faults nor acquires solid virtues. For
such an individual, spiritual exercises have become an end
in themselves, and he performs them merely to satisfy his
conscience.

The result is a deadening sense of routine. There can be
no transformation because there is no energy to effect
change. Without the motivation for progress it is impossible
to succeed spiritually. Consequently, the individual must
set up goals for himself and, forgetting what is behind, must
"press on towards the goal, to the prize of God's heavenly
call in Christ Jesus" (Phil. 3:14).

When such motivation is operative, cognitive patterns
may be developed. Psychologically, the function of such
patterns or frames of reference is adjustment to a complex
environment. The individual often short-cuts volitional
processes by utilization of certain habitual (semi-conscious) cognitive patterns which consequently facilitate
choice. This eliminates the strain of continual intellectual
decisions and repeated evaluations.[6] The Catholic, for example, does not have to decide each Sunday whether or not
he is going to remain a Catholic. His behavior, attending
Mass, is regulated by certain cognitive patterns built up
through past experience. Although there are obvious advantages, such semi-conscious cognitions may be based on
no rational choice at all, but may merely be the result of
the unconscious assimilation of a naturalistic orientation.
The same Catholic may go to Mass merely because of social
pressures. And the individual in religious life may act for
similar, natural motives.

[6] Frederick Bartlett, *Thinking* (New York: Basic Books, 1958), pp.
174–175.

There is nothing quite so difficult as the discipline of standing still and encountering oneself. For the person who wishes to develop a desired cognitive pattern, psychologists recommend deliberate, rational behavior instead of impulsive, irrational activity. The individual must learn to test his reasoning for inconsistencies, to label irrational emotional responses to persons and situations, and to trace vague anxieties to specific problem areas.[7] This is, in effect, to render the unconscious conscious. In this way the unconscious pressures which propel a person to compulsive activity and the attitudes which hinder his spiritual growth come to light and may be regulated.

Specifically, the individual in religious life must repeatedly examine himself to ascertain the extent of secularistic patterns of thought, and the extent of those which represent, not his own convictions, but attitudes unconciously assimilated from the minority of individuals whose spiritual ideals are inferior and who generate the "crowd spirit." Unless the religious man constantly guards against these influences, there will be no progress, no transformation; and the crisis of integrity will remain unresolved.

In addition to these continual examinations and evaluations, the individual must learn to draw profit from the experiences of life. Many events may operate to bring about a beneficial change in a person's frame of reference.[8] It may be the inspiring example of a truly holy person, the contact with suffering which serves to draw a person out of egocentric isolation, or the experience of being loved by another person. In fact, this capacity to learn from an experience—to examine and understand it, and to apply the

[7] John Dollard and Neal E. Miller, *Personality and Psychotherapy* (New York: McGraw-Hill, 1950), p. 437.

[8] Karen Horney, *Our Inner Conflicts* (New York: Norton, 1945), p. 240.

insight to life—is often a sign of docility to the inspiration
of grace. But prerequisite to such a capacity is the capacity
for silence.

If the goal of religious transformation is the possession of
the mind of Christ to the exclusion of naturalistic and materialistic orientations, if the religious man is to attain such
ego integrity, there are no better means of attaining this
end than the traditional silence which ideally pervades the
religious house and the consequent spirit of recollection
which this silence ideally engenders in the individual. In
fact, it is often said that all that is needed to reform a
mediocre religious community is that the rule of silence be
perfectly observed. The same is true for the individual: "If
any man think himself to be religious, not bridling his
tongue but deceiving his own heart, this man's religion is
vain" (James 1:26).

This is a basic point of contrast between the natural and
the supernatural mentality. The man of the world is cordial
and articulate. He has learned the skill of not allowing gaps
of silence to impede the steady conversational flow. The
man of God, however, realizes that every real word rises
from silence. The man of the world seeks contact with other
men. The religious man seeks contact with God and then
with other men. In a world threatened by the herd-instinct
and the pursuit of action for action's sake, the building of
individual worlds of silence and recollection is a necessity,
but requires, as Dostoevski said, a great talent.

Ultimately, the process of religious transformation is
identical with the process of recollection. Gabriel Marcel[9]
has written that it is within recollection that man becomes

[9] Gabriel Marcel, *The Philosophy of Existence* (New York: Philosophical Library, 1949), p. 12.

capable of establishing his position in regard to his life. It is here that he resolves the crisis of integrity and avoids the dangers that failure to resolve this crisis poses to his maturity.

To be recollected is simply to live so strongly on faith that things and people are seen as Jesus Christ would see them. Impelled by the desire to return love for love, the religious man strives to commit himself entirely to Christ and to think as He thought. This cognitive reconstruction—the work of developing authentically Christian habits of thought—becomes possible when there is concomitantly the motivational force of a generous love. Secular and materialistic patterns of thought are then eradicated and spiritual patterns substituted. The individual escapes the subtle leveling process which sometimes occurs within the religious community because he has developed convictions of his own and is therefore capable of achieving a healthy independence of "the crowd."

He will defend his convictions against any attack made upon them because they are convictions gained with grace through prayer and recollection. They are prized because they have been won with difficulty: "For my thoughts are not your thoughts, nor your ways my ways, saith the Lord. For as the heavens are exalted above the earth, so are my ways exalted above your ways, and my thoughts above your thoughts" (Isaias 55:8–9). Prayer bridges an infinite gulf; and, because the thoughts of God are assimilated only gradually and with great effort, they are not quickly surrendered.

Christ commanded the waves to be still, and they obeyed Him. The man of the world refuses to obey and is lost in a whirlpool of noise and commotion. The man of God must be still, for only within stillness is transformation possible.

Faith must be remade moment by moment through the reiterated decision to cut off the noise of the world. With
grace, a perfect transformation, a mature ego integrity may
be attained.

Prayer

7 No discussion of the spiritual development of the religious man is complete without some mention of the growth process which ideally occurs in his prayer. Here, of course, there is a wide range of individual differences. Yet, although they differ greatly in the specific details of their prayer-life, individuals generally show a very similar developmental trend. Here again it will perhaps prove useful to make several applications based upon human cognitive psychology.

It is necessary first, however, to distinguish formal and informal prayer. Formal prayer refers typically to that prayer which is made at a specific time in the daily life of the religious man. Informal prayer, on the other hand, has no specific time and is simply the attempt to live constantly in the presence of God.

It is in such prayer, formal and informal, that the religious man finds himself, his identity, and ultimately perfect integrity. In the light of prayer one's selfhood is revealed, and grace operates to effect transformation and assimilation into Christ: "In Him was life, and the life was the light of men" (John 1:4).

The enterprise of prayer requires cooperation between God and man. Since God always does His part in this mutual enterprise, the burden is man's. Principally, he has the duty of cultivating three cognitive states or attitudes—

the attitude of quiet, that of generosity, and that of perseverance.

We tend to think of silence as the elimination of noise,
although it is actually noise which eliminates silence. At
the heart of all of man's greatest accomplishments there is
always silence. This is even more necessarily the case when
man is confronting his God and his own selfhood.

But quiet is not merely an external state, a physical condition. It is primarily a psychological condition, a condition
of calm, of peace. In this sense, the term *quiet* is more
generic and connotes both interior and exterior silence. It
connotes a total attitude or posture of relaxation in which,
as Guardini puts it, the convulsions of the will are stilled,
the restlessness of the struggle is quieted, and the shrieking
of desire silenced.

It is in moments of quiet that man rediscovers his own
identity and reaffirms his particular life style. Without such
periods there is diffusion. This is the first crisis associated
with prayer. It centers in the question of quiet. It presents
man with the alternative: to set aside, as a permanent, essential part of the day, a time for quiet, for concentration
upon himself and his relation to God—or to close off silence,
to suffocate silence with noise, and to suffer consequent
self-diffusion.

The attitude of quiet requires courage. In the moment of
silence man confronts a demanding God. There is an
almost irresistible tendency for man to turn and flee. He
welcomes any divergency, any little noise, any foreign activity to divert his attention from the voice and claims of
God. Unless he generously withstands himself, his own
impulse to flee, he risks failure in his effort to pray.

Rilke said that everything that is great is difficult. There
is in prayer a certain fear of the unknown. Yet personality,
in its highest moment, is essentially generous. It is outgoing

and liberal, the exact converse of static security. If man is to attain the fullness of his personality, he must overcome his fear.

This is the second crisis associated with prayer. It is the crisis connected with generosity and the willingness to undergo transformation. The individual who fears to adapt himself, his life, to the will of God runs the risk of spiritual inertia. For prayer is merely a means to attain the end of the spiritual life—a perfect concordance of will with the will of God. In prayer, the will of God is discovered, and from prayer the strength and grace to fulfill that will derive.

The third attitude of the man of prayer is the attitude of perseverance. It was this attitude more than any other that Christ demanded of His followers in their prayer. In fact, from the Gospel texts, it appears almost as if this was Christ's only recommendation about prayer. He repeated it constantly in many different parables, all of which pressed home this same lesson—that prayer must be made with persevering courage.

This involves its own crisis—that which could terminate in discouragement and an eventual resignation to mediocrity. The religious man faces the alternative of continuing a seemingly unrewarding prayer, or of abandoning prayer altogether. Often it would seem that the time set aside for prayer could be employed much more profitably for apostolic purposes. If the individual does not give up prayer entirely, he may compromise by continuing halfheartedly and without enthusiasm. But such a compromise is itself a failure. The only successful resolution of this crisis is prayer made perseveringly and energetically.

If these three attitudes—quiet, generosity, and perseverance—are fostered by the religious man, there is the possibility of progress in prayer. If, however, the crisis attending the adoption of each of these attitudes is not resolved, there is no progress and consequently regression.

In addition, there are other crises at another level. These concern certain practical problems in prayer. Even when a person's attitudes toward prayer are otherwise well-established, it is possible for him to find himself incapable of solving the practical difficulties involved in prayer.

Distractions, for example, are a constant source of annoyance to the religious man. They infiltrate his prayer and prevent him from attaining its primary goal, which is union with God. For distractions are distractions even if they are about holiness. They take the person out of the presence of God and turn prayer into a monologue.

If one is to overcome the problem of distractions, a serious effort must be made to discipline patterns of thought—especially outside of the time for prayer. All thoughts must be held within bounds. A project or an idea should be allowed to absorb attention up to a point and no farther. And in prayer distractions should be handled realistically. They can serve to bring the individual humbly back to God with a greater conviction of his unworthiness. Often they may be turned into prayer. The person may find it helpful merely to stop and pray about what is causing the distraction.

Fatigue and weariness also present practical problems. They pull the individual away from God and make prayer often seem impossible. The individual may be overworked through no fault of his own; and when he comes to prayer, he may find it impossible to overcome his human nature.

But it is easy to be deceived in this matter. Only when the individual is certain that he has done his part to overcome weariness can he find consolation in the words of St. Paul: "I will glory in my infirmities, that the strength of Christ may dwell in me" (2 Cor. 12:9). He must have the guarantee that he has endeavored to inure his body on other occasions so that it does not become accustomed to obtaining all the comforts it seeks. This requires a constant mortification and continual watchfulness.

When these and other practical difficulties are surmounted, at least to some extent, and when the individual has achieved the positive attitudes required for prayer, growth becomes possible. Natural, psychological patterns and the ordinary workings of grace interact as the prayer-life of the individual develops.

Progress in prayer follows in its development the natural channels of human cognitive development. For progress in prayer is primarily progress in faith and love, and these supernatural virtues are rooted ultimately in the operations of man's intellect and will. Consequently, it is logical to assume that the prayer of the man of God, as a growth process, passes through phases and changes which parallel those occurring in any process of cognitive and affective development. The grace of God operates in conjunction with these natural laws, finally bringing the natural to its supernatural fulfillment.

In any development of human knowledge there is initially a moment of perception, without which there is no possibility of cognition. Simultaneously, a process of assimilation of information occurs. There is a gradual integration and correlation of factual data. In becoming acquainted with another person, for example, a man notes certain features—expressions, mannerisms, facial characteristics, tone of voice, biographical information. This initial period of observation and discovery is ordinarily pleasing because of its novelty and because of the sense of surprise that accompanies it.

But the novelty and surprise pass. Without the individual

being aware of it, his knowledge of the other person gradually reduces itself to a coherent whole, to a totality, to what the psychologists call the perception of a "Gestalt." Consequently, the mention of the name of the other person recalls to mind a generalized, somewhat differentiated, although perhaps vague, awareness of that person. This knowledge, of course, becomes more and more differentiated and specific as time goes on, but the total process is one of gradual simplification. The individual does not have to continue a detailed study of general characteristics. Old acquaintances are readily differentiated.

The same process occurs in scientific knowledge. There is initially a period of surprise, of fresh enthusiasm, as the individual enters the study of some field. Broad, general lines of thought are developed and pursued. The novelty of the knowledge is intrinsically satisfying. Gradually, the whole, the "Gestalt," is rounded out. An overview has been acquired. The field, in some limited sense, has been "mastered."

In prayer, the process is similar. Initially, there is the period of discovery, of discursive meditation. This is the time when the truths of faith are encountered in the books of the Old and New Testament, in the Person of Christ, and in the teaching of the Church. There is a large element of surprise here as the individual becomes aware for the first time of the meaning of truths to which he formerly had paid mere lip service. There is a new insight, such as that which the child experiences at the first moment when he realizes that two and two do make four.

Gradually, as this new knowledge is assimilated and reduced to a coherent whole, to a succinct and concise picture of reality, the novelty and freshness disappear. The process, of course, varies considerably for different individuals.

Many persons who enter religious life have already completed the work of fashioning this total view of spiritual reality. For these it is a mistake to insist on analytic and discursive meditation. Others may not acquire such knowledge for many years. But, generally speaking, there eventually comes a time when it is futile to continue a rather discursive study of sacred truths. The individual's natural, intellectual grasp of religious beliefs has reached a state of relative permanence. There is no longer the pleasure of discovery.

Although it is, of course, never entirely absent from prayer in the earlier phase, greater affection is characteristic of this second phase. The individual has acquired the ability to pass swiftly from one thought to another. His knowledge is no longer a series of fragmentized and disassociated truths, but rather a single intuition with various dimensions and subdimensions which oscillate in importance as grace dictates. Now it is possible for the individual to perceive the ramifications and connections between the various parts of the whole, and such deepened knowledge leads to greater and greater love.

In the development of the individual's prayer it is generally true that simplified awareness of the truths of revelation and of the personality of Christ is accompanied by an emotional and affective state of warmth and joy. The analogy here is to the feeling of the individual who has "mastered" a given area of science. But like the state of the person studying science, this feeling is generally illusory. The joy is superficial and premature. The individual studying science gradually comes to realize that his knowledge is at all points incomplete. He has grasped a certain totality, but each of the parts requires years of specialized study. On the affective side, the individual in prayer comes to

realize that this initial emotional feeling lacks depth. There
is a great difference between this premature "consolation"
and real spiritual joy.

Gradually, the shallowness of this prayer becomes manifest. Emotional resolutions are enthusiastically multiplied
But they have no real bearing on daily living. The individual
becomes disappointed with himself, and the self-love and
pride concealed behind this disappointment create a serious
danger to spiritual growth. Slowly, the affective element in
prayer becomes less pronounced, intensifying the crisis.
Soon the individual finds himself almost entirely unable to
pray—or at least to pray in the way in which he was previously accustomed to pray.

At this point the individual is ready to enter a new stage
in the development of his prayer-life. He has passed
through the stages of discursive meditation and affective
prayer. He has exhausted the emotional delights of prayer,
and now experiences a certain boredom and sensible dis-
taste when it is time for formal prayer. This is an indica-
tion, paradoxically, that he is advancing.

However, it must be pointed out once more that these
stages in development are of the most general sort, and that
there is a wide range of individual variation. Often the
first two stages—of discursive meditation and affective
prayer—are closely associated with each other. For some
individuals the third phase in the cycle—this apparent
paralysis that overcomes the individual when he prays—
occurs early in the process of his growth. For others it is a
late development.

Again, the present phase in the individual's development
in prayer is best understood when an analogy is drawn to
certain cognitive processes. One of the most important
moments in the cognitive development of the child comes

when he grasps an abstract idea. He may be looking intensely at two blocks and suddenly realize that they are "two." Or he may eventually come to understand the meaning of "round" or "blue" or "man," disengaging the abstract concept from its concrete manifestations.

In a certain sense all education consists in this process of moving from the concrete to the abstract, from the material to the spiritual. The child learns to read by becoming able to untangle the meaning of a word from its printed appearances. But such a process involves an abstraction, a withdrawal of attention from the particular style of print and a focusing upon the content revealed through the printed symbols.

In prayer a similar process of abstraction occurs. The individual must move from a natural to a supernatural understanding of revealed truth. Gradually faith must play a more and more predominant rôle in the individual's prayer. And this requires a purification or abstraction from a natural mental grasp of truth. The individual finds his natural powers in a state of apparent paralysis. There is no delight in prayer; there are no insights; there is only a strong abhorrence of prayer. (This, of course, presupposes that the person is otherwise well-disposed and that he possesses the proper attitudes toward prayer—in short, that he is mortified and trying to pray.)

In such a state the individual's prayer is the prayer of faith.[1] It is now a more specifically supernatural activity. There has been a progressive whittling away or "abstraction" of the natural, until bare faith alone remains. The individual may experience either the consolation of knowing that God is indescribably close or may feel desolation because of the apparent absence of God. The intensity of

[1] Leonard Boase, S.J., *The Prayer of Faith* (Wimbleton: Apostleship of Prayer, 1950), pp. 50–51.

these experiences differs greatly among individuals, and for
one person there may be continual fluctuations from one
extreme to the other.

Gradually, however, the presence of God becomes more
and more apparent to the individual. Of course, the Christian always assents by faith to the presence of God, but now
this faith is being purified and made more comprehensible,
more personally meaningful. There are two moments in this
process, one negative and the other positive.

The negative constituent is that previously mentioned:
the interference of intellectual and imaginative activities
and the diminution of the emotional or affective element in
prayer. The early phases of the developmental cycle of the
individual's prayer were characterized by a strong intellectual and emotional content. Now these are noticeably
absent. Human consciousness is being adapted to a supernatural mode of knowledge.

The absence of God can be experienced during this phase
in agonizing intensity. Distractions multiply, and the individual finds himself unable to concentrate. He feels that he
is doing nothing, that nothing is happening. Prayer apparently is a waste of time. And precisely because the
individual is experiencing a new, supernatural mode of
knowledge, no satisfaction is given to the natural powers
previously employed in prayer. This is why, traditionally,
such a phase in the religious man's development has been
called a "night."

Positively, however, there is an increasing experiential
awareness of the presence of God. There are fluctuations
and oscillations in the intensity of the sense of God's presence, but the dominant direction is toward a greater awareness of God, of the fact that God exists, and of His presence
in the individual's soul. Prayer slowly simplifies until all
that remains is this intuitive awareness of God's presence.

And there is also a change in the individual's love. For although each phase in the development of the life of prayer is most readily distinguished on the basis of changes in knowledge, there are also distinguishable changes in the person's love. These are changes in the intensity, but also in the quality, of love. However, such changes are not perceived as readily as those that occur in the individual's way of knowing. In general, the operations of the Holy Spirit upon man's soul through grace are not experienced sensibly by the person. Nevertheless, it is often true that during this phase in prayer, simultaneous with the general diminution of natural activity within the sphere of consciousness, there is a gradual diminution of emotional elements in love. The individual comes to love God more, but to feel it less.

Another important change can be observed, not so much in the quality of love as in the individual's evaluative judgments. He comes to prize things, to see the world, in terms of the supernatural. He gradually learns the difficult though obvious lesson that God is beyond all relation or proportion to anything and everything else. Slowly the person acquires a spiritual frame of reference. He begins to think, and consequently to will, as God thinks and wills.

Willing is normally proportioned to knowing. Love depends on knowledge. A man cannot love a person whom he does not know—at least it is impossible to love such a person in any other than the most general way. And it is also necessary that human love be free. It must be spontaneous, not a payment for a debt or a return on a loan.

But man's knowledge of God is meager and inadequate, and were his love conformed to this knowledge, it would be wholly insufficient. For creatures are known more directly and hence would be loved more than the Creator. Moreover, man's freedom is jeopardized because of the relationship in which he stands to God. Man has no freedom when

it is a question of loving what is intrinsically infinite Goodness. God, through the perfect and irresistible attractiveness
of His Being, would compel man's love unless He had
found a way in which man could love Him freely and yet
directly. This is the way of faith.

In faith man reaches God Himself. Yet he remains essentially free in this vision and is not necessarily moved by
God's perfection because he sees dimly and with human
eyes. God is obscure and yet revealed, hidden and yet manifest. Through faith man can love God with a love out of
proportion to the inadequate conception of Him that the
human mind possesses. In this case willing is disproportionate to knowing. Consequently, through faith love transcends
knowledge. Man's knowledge of God ends with unknowing,
and from this starting point love grows, gradually becoming
transformed into the divine Charity itself.

Sown in baptism, the seed of faith grows as the young
child becomes acquainted with the content of revelation
and the teachings of the Church. Gradually this knowledge
matures and its roots sink deeper into the layers of personality. The person learns to see the image and reflection
of God in His creation—until the immediate, experiential
presence of God in the soul becomes the one overpowering
reality that shapes and determines his orientation toward
life. In a similar way the fire of charity is kindled in baptism, gradually mounts in childhood and youth, and finally
is transformed and coalesces with the consuming Charity of
God, the love of the Spirit who is the eternal love of the
Father and the Son.

The developmental process generally characteristic of the
life of prayer follows, therefore, a path of progressive simplification. There is a contraction of knowledge and an
expansion of love, until the one overriding fact of consciousness is the presence of God. The more mystical stages

follow as a deeper and deeper understanding of the essence of God develops with a corresponding increase in love.

Developmentally, the phases of informal prayer parallel those of formal prayer. In the beginning the habit of ejaculatory prayer and the practice of the presence of God are deliberately fostered. Gradually these acts become more affective, and the individual becomes increasingly capable of seeing the events and happenings of the day in a spirit of faith. Supernatural habits develop until the religious man lives in God who "is not far from any one of us. For in Him we live and move and have our being" (Acts 17:27–28).

Psychologically, the abiding awareness of the presence of God amid a multitude of other thoughts entertained during the day seems impossible. One object only can clearly and explicitly occupy the field of consciousness at a given instant. However, it is possible to hold several thoughts in the mind at one time in different ways. Two objects can be present in consciousness at the same time, although at differing intensities of consciousness. The memory of one thought may constantly influence the individual's thinking and acting, but may only come into consciousness when the person has ceased attending to other objects. The classic example of this is that of the mother who is motivated in all she does by the thought of her sick child, although totally absorbed in other occupations. As soon as she is free from these other duties, her thoughts immediately return to her sick child.

The example is useful because it points out that such a state is natural, and is not to be attained by conscious straining and anxious effort. It is merely the result of a strong love. Similarly, there is no extraordinary gift required to come to that habitual state in which the presence

of God is constantly close to awareness. Grace, of course, is
necessary, but primarily as a help to achieve the state of
mortification and detachment that is essential to the practice of recollection. The example of the mother who thinks
of her sick child habitually, even while engrossed in other
occupations, points out the compelling force of an intense
love.[2]

Prompted by such love, the religious man develops facility in the practice of finding God in all things. Here again
there is need for quiet, generosity, and perseverance. The
religious man must be quietly attentive to the rhythm of
God that beats in creation. Such recollectedness does not
imply that he withdraws from his daily occupations. True
recollection consists in attaining a certain interior quiet
which does not banish thoughts of everyday matters, but
which considers all things in the spirit of faith.

Generosity and perseverance are necessary for constancy
in this prayer and in the continual renewal that it necessitates. There must be a generous movement away from that
form of attachment to things which holds the religious man
back from God and makes it difficult for him to perceive
God's action in creatures and in events. And the religious
man must persevere in the effort to foster a contemplative
attitude—one in which the bread that he eats, the weather,
his health, even his own misfortunes and those of others
are seen as gifts of God.

While it has been compared to the behavior of the artist
who stares at a horizon or a flower, the contemplation
which eventually should come to characterize the formal
prayer of the religious man is not a mental staring. There
are oscillations in attention, but in this constant flux one

[2] Joseph de Guibert, S.J., *The Theology of the Spiritual Life* (New
York: Sheed and Ward, 1953), pp. 252–253.

idea retains a predominant position. This idea and the various aspects of it that are isolated and considered are objects of contemplation, while the other thoughts that occur are distractions. A strong emotional tone characterizes this process, and in this sense the dialogue and silence of contemplation resemble that of two lovers. There is both perception and affection. The individual moves from one aspect to another, perceiving the goodness of the beloved. Affective prayer, like the conversation of lovers, expresses, maintains, and elicits love.[3]

In the informal prayer of recollection, contemplation consists primarily in an effort of direction. Instead of turning to men and things simply, the individual turns them to God. In this sense the whole of everyday life becomes a prayer. The inconsiderateness of youth, the weariness and inevitable opinionatedness of old age, monotonous hours of work, physical discomfort—these and all the trials and sufferings of life can be made prayer. But the same is true of the joys and blessings of life as well. Everything can be sanctified, and is sanctified through the attitude of contemplation.

Quite simply, such an attitude is fostered—positively— by the effort to practice the virtues, to love God in one's daily activities, and to look for His will and His action in all things. Negatively, the individual becomes disposed to contemplation by avoiding occasions of dissipation, by mortifying his senses, and by withdrawing from any form of discursive and analytic prayer when drawn by grace to a more simple exercise of attention and recollection.

This last point is of central importance since so many individuals are hindered from making progress in their prayer-life because of an irrational rigidity which fears

[3] G. Augustine Ellard, S.J., "Contemplation the Terminus of Mental Prayer," *Review for Religious*, 7 (1948), 226.

change. Unless this fear is overcome, there is a grave danger
that prayer will be abandoned because the individual is
unwilling to pray in any way other than discursively. For
in the normal course of events such discursive prayer becomes distasteful and quite unpleasing after a time and
must yield to a simpler and more affective prayer. The
same is true of the practice of recollection where the habit
of spontaneous affective prayer and a generally supernatural outlook should replace what initially was a highly
deliberate and somewhat artificial practice of ejaculatory
prayer and acts of God's presence. These changes are to be
expected merely on the basis of the natural development of
man's cognitive powers. If the individual is resistant to this
natural and supernatural growth process, he clogs the workings of grace and frustrates God's plan.

When he prays, man is never alone. The Christian prays
as a member of the Church. Historically, the Greek notion
of contemplation—alone with the Alone—prevailed for
centuries over the social notion of contemplation. But such
a social notion is inherent in the Christian faith.

The prayer of the Christian may demand external solitude, but he carries within himself the interests and needs
of the whole Church. These may concern him only re-
motely, but they are his specific duty. He has an account to
render for them personally. Consequently, the individual is
obliged to acquaint himself with the functions of the
Church and to submit his own will to the Church's needs.
He must make proper use of the time allotted him for
prayer and discipline himself so that he corresponds to the
inspiration of grace in as perfect a manner as is possible.
These are social, not merely personal, obligations.

The individual is loved by Christ in His Church. The
Church is the bride of Christ, and its members share in the

love of Christ for His bride. The individual does not abandon his personality or become absorbed into the totality.
Rather he retains his individuality and renders to the
Bridegroom an alert and diligent, personal service of love.
For the Church is not just a social organization or a super-
structure which submerges individual personalities. The
Church is not an abstraction—a theology, an ethics, or an
institution. Nor is the Church a kind of lifestream surging
from the roots up into the branches. Any analogy to natural
life gives merely one aspect of the Church's unity.

The Church is a living unity of unique persons upon
whom, in whom, and out of whom the Spirit operates. The
life of the Church does not threaten to absorb the lives of
its members, but rather brings them to God and so to the
fulfillment of their own uniqueness. Whenever a man confronts the living God in faith and love as a member of the
one bride of Christ, the Church, the divine uniqueness is
reflected from the Word and falls upon him. No analogy in
the natural order adequately clarifies this mystery. It must
be experienced and known of itself through the Church's
life in the individual and the individual's life in the
Church.[4]

Dostoevski was greatly impressed by the widespread belief of the Russian people of his time that the earth continues to exist only in virtue of the fact that its holiness
never fails—that somewhere, in the desert, unknown and
unheralded, there are a few holy men.

The Church, the bride of Christ, has many parts and a
multiplicity of functions. But the one supreme obligation
of the Church is that of perpetuating holiness on the earth.
The best Christians are not necessarily the learned or the

[4] Hans Urs von Balthasar, *Prayer* (New York: Sheed and Ward, 1961), pp. 76–77.

influential. The leaders of Christianity are not necessarily those whose voices resound in the public square or in the press. The actions of the best Christians usually go unnoticed. They live lives that are hidden from the world. The famous reformer, the influential churchman, the leader of nations—these may also be great saints. But many saints are known only after death, and many are never known to the men of this world. And it is in and through them that the Church achieves its mission of preserving holiness in the world.

The religious man contracts this obligation to holiness as a necessary consequence of his mode of life. He necessarily commits himself to the enterprise of sanctification. It is not merely a personal enterprise, since it has social reverberations in the Church. But it is a call to personal sacrifice and dedication. For such an individual, as Leon Bloy said, the only tragedy is not to be a saint.

And sanctity consist simply in union with God. In the hours of his formal prayer and in the practice of recollection, the religious man consolidates this union. Gradually he comes to think God's thoughts after Him and to see in creation the infinite Goodness of the Creator. For all things, as Gerard Manley Hopkins pointed out, are charged with God and, if man knows how to touch them, give off sparks and take fire, telling of Him. But the problem comes in learning how to touch creation.

The ability to find God in all things is an art and consequently must, under grace, be developed. The individual must cooperate with grace and with his own human nature. The developmental processes, psychological and spiritual, which normally characterize formal and informal prayer have been sketched briefly in the preceding pages. There is, of course, room for considerable variation among persons or in the life of one person. But, generally speaking, the process of grace is one of progressive simplification and purification, until the individual attains the attitude of contemplation through which he structures the universe so that all creatures come to be seen as graces of God.[5]

In one of his novels, Paul Horgan described an old French missionary dying of snake-bite in the Mexican desert. Slowly and painfully he murmured the words of the *Magnificat* as he lay under the desert sun: "My soul magnifies the Lord." Even death could not prevent what had become habitual to him. "And my spirit rejoices in God my Savior," he said without knowing that he spoke. But he brought a life of prayer with him to death's door, and in a little while it entered with him.[6]

[5] Louis Lavelle, *The Meaning of Holiness* (New York: Pantheon, 1951), p. 64.

[6] Paul Horgan, *The Devil in the Desert* (New York: Longmans, Green, 1952), p. 58.

Conclusion

It is thoroughly misleading to conceive of the religious life as something static. Generally speaking, current ascetical writing stresses the dynamic aspects of spiritual life. In treating of the virtues of the religious state, these writings give much attention to processes involved in their development and cultivation, rather than to an objectified analysis or classification according to their types and subtypes.

Recent interest in psychology and a new awareness of the important rôle psychological processes play in the spiritual development of the individual have stimulated this study of the dynamic factors involved in religious growth. While cautioning against an overly psychological, and hence natural, approach which leaves little room for the movement of grace, the current literature of ascetical psychology is premised upon the maxim that grace builds upon nature.

This book follows in the same tradition, emphasizing especially the interaction of psychological and spiritual developmental processes. The theory of "ego epigenesis," formulated by Erik H. Erikson, has been employed, not dogmatically, but rather pragmatically, as pointing up processes in the normal psychological growth pattern which are of use as a general framework in discussing the spiritual development of the religious man. The psychoanalytic side of the theory has been deliberately played down as well as the emphasis which Erikson places, for methodological purposes, upon abnormal and extreme phenomena (since he feels that these represent the normal case "writ large").

The theory, then, merely provides a conceptual frame of reference and a starting point for discussion. Its constructs are not to be understood as ontologically given. Like any theory, Erikson's schematization of the developmental process is merely a form of scientific shorthand to facilitate analysis. The different stages and phases in the life cycle may vary for individuals in their length, in the intensity of the crisis they pose, even in their presence or absence. There may be, and most probably are, overlaps between the different phases and crises.

But, for the most part, the theory reflects the typical process of psychological growth which culminates, ideally, in adult maturity. And, for purposes of analysis, the theory is helpful since it segments conceptually what is actually a steady developmental flow and thus allows discussion of dynamic forces, both psychological and spiritual, operative in the formation and transformation of the religious man. Typically, these forces interact in this process, though they may, of course, affect the individual singly.

By way of summary—and to give unity to the previous discussion—it will perhaps help to review the various dimensions of identity formation. Erikson regards the process of identity formation (as distinct from the identity crisis) as a lifetime process transcending and yet involving all of the phases of the developmental cycle. It is not resolved once and for all at any one stage in development, but rather is successfully and perfectly achieved only at the termination of the process.

Each of the different stages in the developmental cycle marks off a different period and a different crisis in the process of identity formation. The derivatives of earlier

phases in the cycle and the precursors of future crises are
also operative during any given stage. In the lives of adults,
the psychosocial quality of earlier stages in development
becomes more differentiated as the personality evolves.
Consequently, the residuals of early achievements, when
viewed at a later stage, are relative to that stage and must
be reconsidered accordingly. Basic trust, for example, is a
good and fundamental quality of personality, but its psychosocial quality differs in the child and in the adult.[1]

The identity of the religious man has a specific character
to it, and the process of identity formation is in his case
only accomplished in, through, and with Christ. This is the
essence of his commitment: "If then any man is in Christ,
he is a new creature: the former things have passed away;
behold they are made new" (2 Cor. 5:17). And the acquisition of this new identity in Christ is a lifetime process—one
terminating only at death. In this sense it runs parallel to
and forms the supernatural counterpart of the natural,
psychological process of identity formation.

For the religious man each stage represents a gradual
deepening in his understanding and love of Christ, and
comprises one of a series of successive steps in the total
process of transformation. Each has, similarly, its own crisis
and each is influenced by the past and the future. Moreover, in the adult religious person the residuals of each of
the earlier stages play an important part and contribute
their own essential elements to the fullness of his maturity.

"He who sees Me, sees Him who sent Me" (John 12:45).
The life of Christ reveals to man in human terms the mystery of the Divinity. Christ is God's likeness on earth. To
know Christ is to know God. But Christ is not merely God,
He is also man. The Son of God continually referred to

[1] Erik H. Erikson, *Identity and the Life Cycle* (New York: International University Press, 1959), p. 141.

Himself as the Son of Man. Man's situation is so lowly and
God's purpose for him is so great that God elevated human
nature. In Christ, man becomes the possessor of unlimited
potentialities. In Him alone can man attain to perfect and
mature humanity. This is why Dostoevski said that he
could not conceive of humanity apart from Christ. Christ
has fully entered into humanity, and man must strive to
transform himself into the Person of Christ as his ideal.

To be human, then, to be perfectly mature, is not something that happens automatically or merely through a
process of physical maturation and growth. It also involves
both a psychological and a spiritual process, a development
along natural and supernatural dimensions. It is the result
of a process of growth in Christ. In the pages of the Gospel
the religious man discovers what trust, autonomy, initiative,
and the various other dimensions of identity formation
mean, psychologically and spiritually, in his adult life.

In the words of Christ's Sermon on the Mount the religious man discovers the meaning of a mature sense of
trust: "Therefore I say to you, do not be anxious for your
life, what you shall eat; nor yet for your body, what you
shall put on" (Matt. 6:25). Christ's own life perfectly exemplified this attitude of detachment from the goods of
creation. Christ taught His followers by word and by action
the important lesson that God is a loving Father who will
not fail to care for those who walk before Him with child-
like trust. "The foxes have dens, and the birds of the air
have nests, but the Son of Man has nowhere to lay His
head" (Luke 9:58). The lesson of trust is quite evident in
Christ's life, but it is so contrary to the thinking of modern
man that it is usually ignored.

The development of such a sense of trust, however, is the
basic inspiration of the poverty of the religious man. The

individual attempts to achieve through grace a spirit of detachment from created things. Yet he is concomitantly aware of the goodness and beauty of creatures. Perhaps quite purposively, at the same time that He spoke to His disciples of a spirit of trusting detachment, Christ pointed out the beauty of creation: "See how the lilies of the field grow; they neither toil nor spin, yet I say to you that not even Solomon in all his glory was arrayed like one of these" (Matt. 6:28–29).

A mature sense of trust, therefore, includes a childlike confidence, a spirit of poverty and detachment, and a healthy appreciation of the blessings of life and the goodness of God. The crisis that threatens to terminate in mistrust is most fundamentally characteristic of infancy, but the religious man must, in a certain sense and on a quite different level, relive this crisis before he can attain to the fullness of his maturity. At various moments in his life, under certain circumstances, the individual's sense of trust will be endangered. For some persons this may be the most important stage in their development. For others the mature crisis of trust may be minimal.

Any solution that the religious man discovers for this crisis is reducible ultimately to that of Christ: "Therefore do not be anxious, saying, 'What shall we eat?' or, 'What shall we drink?' or, 'What are we to put on?' (for after all these things the Gentiles seek); for your Father knows that you need all these things. But seek first the kingdom of God and His justice, and all these things shall be given you besides" (Matt. 6:31–33).

The words of Christ and the example of His life also set before the religious man the ideal of a lasting sense of mature *autonomy*. The individual must come to accept, with its necessary consequences, the psychosocial reality of his own identity. He must learn to stand, actually as a child and figuratively as an adult, on his own two feet.

Christ did not hesitate to assert His Selfhood: "I and the Father are one" (John 10:30). He confronted the Jews with the fact of His Divinity and permitted them to choose to accept or to reject Him. Nor did He hedge His words from fear when He spoke to the Scribes and Pharisees: "Serpents, brood of vipers, how are you to escape the judgment of hell?" (Matt. 23:33). The hand of Christ never trembled. He never showed any signs of doubt in Himself or in His mission.

A pervading doubt and shame are indicative of failure to resolve the crisis of autonomy—either in its infantile form or as a crisis of later development. In religious life the crisis is often intensified by the need for purity of heart and total confidence in God. The awareness of one's human weakness may shake confidence and produce doubt and shame. With grace, however, the individual achieves a successful resolution by grounding his confidence securely upon his personal attachment to Christ and His cause. "My sheep hear My voice, and I know them and they follow Me. And I give them everlasting life" (John 10:27-28). These words bring consolation to the religious man, and also generate a sense of commitment, a spirit of dedication to the mission of Christ's kingdom.

There may be failures, even cowardice. But the individual can profitably utilize even these events—and the moments of crisis they produce—to grow in courage and autonomy. For courage is required to accept with humility the frailty of human nature and to turn again to God with a greater love. And it is the mark of an autonomous person to rise up again and to continue on his own feet when thrown to the ground by the weight of the cross of human weakness. Here once more there is Christ's example.

The fear of failure is heightened, however, in the crisis of *initiative* which characterizes, primarily, childhood and, secondarily, later adult life. Failure to resolve this crisis in any of its forms results in an increased sense of irrational guilt, which consequently inhibits and retards the process of identity formation. Such a sense of guilt arises from painful experiences of childhood or from the failures and setbacks of adult life. It produces a constriction of generosity and prevents the expression of initiative. Resolution of the crisis is achieved by cultivation of a generous love and a mature confidence in oneself and in God.

Apparently, the lives of many of the saints were characterized by a deep and abiding sense of guilt. They seem to be almost preoccupied with the consciousness of the gravity of their sins. In fact, most men find unintelligible the real fear for salvation which the saint feels, his consuming remorse for sins that scarcely seem to be sins at all. The greatest of the saints were moved by a profound sense of their own unworthiness while their contemporaries were revering their sanctity.

Yet the sense of guilt which characterizes the saint is not irrational and psychologically detrimental. It is more humility than guilt. For the saint apprehends the reality of the love of God, and his own unworthiness brings him to his knees in humility. He is continually aware of the breathtaking scope of Divine love and of the infinite gap that separates him from God's holiness. His humility is necessarily excessive in the eyes of other men, but in his own eyes it merely expresses the truth of his situation.

Every man is faced with this choice—the choice of guilt or the choice of humility. The choice of guilt was Judas' choice, and it leads to despair. The choice of humility was Peter's choice, and it leads to love and the mature initiative

of love. This is the significance of Christ's words concerning
the penitent woman: "Her sins, many as they are, shall be
forgiven her, because she has loved much" (Luke 7:47).

In the end man shall be judged on love. This does not
free him from obligation: "Not everyone who says to Me,
'Lord, Lord,' shall enter the kingdom of heaven; but he
who does the will of My Father in heaven shall enter into
the kingdom of heaven" (Matt. 7:21). Rather it imposes
upon man the duty of a loving initiative, a watchful and
enterprising involvement in the mission of the Church.

Closely associated with the sense of initiative is the individual's sense of *industry*. Here again there is a primary
crisis in childhood and its recurrence in similar, although
necessarily modified, crises of adult life. In adulthood, causative factors are typically discouragement, lack of success,
disappointments. The danger of failure to resolve such crises
is paralysis and inferiority. The individual comes to feel
an unrealistic inadequacy which tends to result in inertia.

Again Christ, as the perfect model of human maturity,
exemplifies the individual who has successfully resolved the
problems connected with the crisis of industry. "My Father
works even until now, and I work" (John 5:17). The fullness of His humanity is manifested in His work. Christ
literally toiled for men. Repeatedly the Gospel narrative
tells of His fatigue. He met with failure—"From this time
many of His disciples turned back and no longer went
about with Him" (John 6:67). But He overcame His disappointment and continued working among unappreciative
men. And when He came to the end of His life, He overcame His exhaustion, mounting the cross where He died in
desolation. Christ did not preach comfort, but labor.

There is a particularly important lesson in the labor of
Christ for the religious person. A certain Greek influence

which stresses contemplation to the exclusion of action persists in the tradition of religious life.[2] This is a basically Platonic notion which is manifested in the distrust of worldly affairs and a deliberate cultivation of those that are unworldly. There is a latent conviction, which many individuals entertain, that to be a man of God somehow means to cease to be a man. Instead of throwing themselves into the tasks of life these individuals hold back; and when obedience enjoins upon them such tasks, they feel that the purity of their vocation has been stained.

But such an attitude denies the Incarnation, and ignores Christ sitting at the well of Sichar "wearied from the journey" (John 4:6), or passing through the crowd blessing the children and curing the sick "until the day was far spent" (Mark 6:35), or standing under the hot noonday sun instructing "a great multitude of people from all Judea and Jerusalem, and the sea coast of Tyre and Sidon, who came to listen to Him and to be healed of their diseases" (Luke 6:17–18).

The figure of Christ working among men and involved in the human situation is so compelling that it is easy to forget that this man is God. Yet Christ also exemplifies perfectly a mature sense of *identity*. "The Father is in Me and I in the Father" (John 10:38). There is no conflict. Satan tempted the Son of God with bread but, as He was to tell His apostles, He required but one source of nourishment: "My food is to do the will of Him who sent Me, to accomplish His work" (John 4:34).

The identity of the religious man is also contained in the will of God, in the ideal that God wishes him to attain. In each instance, this ideal is hidden and is only gradually revealed. And in each instance, this ideal is simply Christ

[2] Emerick Coreth, S.J., "Contemplative in Action," *Theological Digest*, 3 (1955), 37–38.

under a new aspect. The religious man does not rigidly imitate the Christ of history, but he seeks to identify himself with Christ so as to act as Christ would act were He in the same circumstances. This requires docility to grace and the assimilation of Christ's mentality in intimate, personal prayer. The goal of such a process of identification is that, through and in man, Christ may complete the work of salvation.

While the attainment of identity is a highly personal enterprise, the religious man will also find that he has contracted a social obligation. Within the Body of Christ which is the Church each of the members plays its own distinct part. "If the whole body were an eye where would be the hearing? If the whole body were hearing, where would be the smelling?" (1 Cor. 12:17). This demands of the individual a new docility—the docility required by obedience. His own identity, like that of Christ, is expressed simply in the perfect exercise of the will of the Father.

Again, it is Christ who exemplifies most perfectly the ideal of mature friendship and love, the sense of *intimacy* of Erikson's theory. In fact, love is the summary of His teaching. The modern secularist constructs the City of Man without love. The Christian would build the City of God on the foundation of Christ's love. Throughout the Gospel there is impressive evidence of this love. Christ is concerned for the crowds "because they were like sheep without a shepherd" (Mark 6:34). He drew little children to Himself and did not allow the disciples to dismiss them: "Let the little children come to Me, and do not hinder them" (Luke 18:16). He wept for Lazarus and for the people of Jerusalem. And in the Garden He longed for the companionship of men.

"And I, if I be lifted up from the earth, will draw all things to Myself" (John 12:32). This was the extent of

Christ's love. The one purpose of His life was to communicate Himself to man, to empty Himself. "Unless the grain of wheat fall into the ground and die, it remains alone. But if it die, it brings forth much fruit" (John 12:24–25). Christ gave Himself totally: "This is My body which is being given for you. . . . This cup is the new covenant in My blood, which shall be shed for you" (Luke 22:19–20). And His love continues in time, extending to all men.

In this love of Christ the religious man finds the source and the model of his own love. His mission to the modern world is to carry Christ's love to men, and to bring man's love to Christ. And in a world where the notion of love has been fundamentally distorted, there is no mission quite so difficult.

Psychologically and spiritually, the religious man initiates his apostolate of love in the genuinely human love of friendship. Here he communicates intimately with another person and learns to supernaturalize human affection by rooting it in his love of God. His model is Christ, and his ideal is the friendship of Christ. For Christ had friends in a real, human sense—and friends who were fishermen. As the person learns to love in the way in which Christ loved, he learns to open himself to all men with the generosity and the vulnerability which characterized Christ's love.

The perfection of love is achieved when the individual has acquired the sense of *generativity*. Love is now of an entirely selfless cast. The individual is concerned with others; he has come to love them more than himself. This is epitomized in the love of Christ. "Greater love than this no one has, that one lay down his life for his friends" (John 15:13). It is characteristic of the special concern Christ showed for those whom His Father committed to Him: "I pray for them; not for the world do I pray, but for those whom Thou hast given Me, because they are Thine; and all things that are Mine are Thine, and Thine are Mine; and I am glorified in them" (John 17:9-10).

Failure to attain this perfection of selflessness entails the danger of self-absorption. The individual becomes preoccupied with himself and his own interests. This is the most serious of the crises of adulthood and, unless it is resolved, the individual is incapable of fulfilling the first law of the new covenant: "These things I command you, that you love one another" (John 15:17). For this love has one essential element, without which it cannot be called Christian, and this is its selflessness.

A second aspect of the generativity crisis concerns the danger of stagnation. This danger is encountered by the religious man in relation to problems connected with his vow of obedience. Obedience carries with it the risk of purposelessness, of a lack of initiative, of indecisiveness. Consequently, it necessitates a lived tension between submission and assertion, between docility and responsibility. This requires openness to grace and the outlook of faith. Again there is the example of Christ: "Father, if Thou art willing, remove this cup from Me; yet not My will but Thine be done" (Luke 22:42). Christ, who spoke with authority and did not hesitate to condemn the Scribes and Pharisees, was in all things submissive to the Father's will.

Integrity is the last of the crises of life. It summarizes the past and relates fundamentally to all that went before. It is in the resolution of this crisis that the fullness of maturity is attained. Failure to achieve a solution may terminate in disgust and despair.

The central direction in the life of the religious person is toward Christ. "I am the way, and the truth, and the life" (John 14:6). Christ is the way to the Father because His life exemplifies the way man is to live. Christ is the truth

of the Father because He speaks as the Father has commanded Him, telling man of God. And Christ is the life of
the Father because His incarnation elevates and dignifies
human nature, restoring man to the life of grace.

Christ exemplified the fullness of personal integrity.
He walked a straight path without deviation or delay. His
guide throughout was the Father's will and His motive the
perfection of love. And He asks the same of His followers:
"You are to be perfect, even as your heavenly Father is perfect" (Matt. 5:48). This is the perfection of the religious
man and this his assurance of integrity: that he performs
the will of God and performs it lovingly.

These are the dimensions of psychological and spiritual
development, considered within the restricted framework
of one theoretical system. There are necessarily inadequacies, but hopefully one dominant theme emerges from
this discussion—that the psychological and the spiritual
interact, that the natural and the supernatural are, in the
practical order at least, interrelated.

Some spiritual writers contend that maturity is prerequisite to sanctity, that grace operates upon nature. Others
maintain that the only path to perfect maturity is that of
holiness. The apparent contradiction of these statements is
resolved by insisting that nature and grace interact. There
are examples of individuals who seemingly arrived at maturity because they achieved high sanctity. Yet there were
saints who showed definite signs of emotional and psychological immaturity. And there are many individuals who
have attained a high degree of psychological and emotional
maturity, but whose spiritual sensitivities remain essentially
immature. Typically, however, the saint is also psychologically well-developed. The exceptions merely serve to point
out more dramatically what is the normal situation. In fact,

the saint is ordinarily more mature than other men—psychologically and spiritually—because he cooperates more perfectly with God who gives and conserves both nature and grace.

The religious person works out his salvation, grows in nature and grace, within the Church, the Mystical Body of Christ. Within the Church and within the essentially spiritual setting it provides, each man plays his own unique rôle and attains his maturity in Christ. "For He Himself gave some men as apostles, and some as prophets, others again as evangelists, and others as pastors and teachers, in order to perfect the saints for a work of ministry, for building up the body of Christ, until we attain to the unity of faith and the depth of knowledge of the Son of God, to perfect manhood, to the mature measure of the fullness of Christ. And this He has done that we may be now no longer children, tossed to and fro and carried about by every wind of doctrine devised by the wickedness of men, in craftiness, according to the wiles of error. Rather we are to practice the truth in love, and so grow up in all things in Him who is the head, Christ" (Eph. 4:11–15).

Index